Praise for *Psychic Witch*

"A harmonious and helpful text to help you grow your own psychic and magickal skills and evolve on the crooked path of the witch."

—Christopher Penczak, author of
the Temple of Witchcraft series

"Mat Auryn crafts compelling prose that shows his caring and dedication to the reader."

—Silver RavenWolf, author of *Solitary Witch*

"If you follow this guide, you will gain access to senses that leave no doubt about the power of magic."

—Jason Miller, author of *The Elements of Spellcrafting*

"An ambitious work that stands at the crossroads where witchcraft, energy work, and psychic development intersect."

—Michelle Belanger, author of *The Psychic Energy Codex*

"Mat is magickally and energetically connected, well-read, and well-researched."

—Laurie Cabot, official witch of Salem and
author of *Power of the Witch*

"A rare jewel that radiates clarity of spirit that is genuinely manifest therein."

—Maxine Sanders, cofounder of the Alexandrian
Tradition of Witchcraft and author of *Firechild*

"The teachings, exercises, and ritual work in this book integrate psychism and magick with ease and grace."

—Ivo Dominguez Jr., cofounder of Assembly of the
Sacred Wheel and author of *The Keys to Perception*

"My only regret is that this book with its treasure trove of magickal exercises was not available when I was first starting out."

—Judika Illes, author of *Encyclopedia of 5000 Spells*

"An excellent and comprehensive guide to awakening any witch's latent abilities."

—Christopher Orapello, cohost on *Down at the Crossroads* podcast and coauthor of *Besom, Stang & Sword*

"This book is a treasure! Mat Auryn illuminates the subtle realm with brilliant clarity."

—Tess Whitehurst, author of *You Are Magical*

"*Psychic Witch* is the most complete source I've ever encountered on the psychic and energetic aspects of magic."

—Madame Pamita, author of *Madame Pamita's Magical Tarot*

"Packed with lore, strategy, and practical tips, *Psychic Witch* is a powerhouse of connecting threads in the world of mental magick."

—David Salisbury, author of *The Deep Heart of Witchcraft*

"Mat Auryn is truly one of the most valuable voices in the witchcraft community today."

—Danielle Dulsky, author of *The Holy Wild*

"By applying these techniques, you are certain to see a monumental change in your perception of your world, and of yourself."

—Chas Bogan, author of *The Secret Keys of Conjure*

"Intuitives and witches alike, you need this book."

—Amy Blackthorn, author of *Blackthorn's Botanical Magic and Sacred Smoke*

"Sure to become a classic of modern witchcraft."

—Cyndi Brannen, author of *True Magic*

"This book is a treasure trove of wisdom."

—Mickie Mueller, author of *The Witch's Mirror*

"If you're interested in developing your psychic abilities right alongside your craft practices, this is the book for you."

—Gwion Raven, author of *The Magick of Food*

"Filled to the brim with hands-on exercises, this book will guide readers through the ins and outs of psychic development and manipulating energy."
—Nicholas Pearson, author of *Stones of the Goddess*

"Mat Auryn provides a rich, accessible course in psychic development and magick."
—Durgadas Allon Duriel, author of *The Little Work*

"*Psychic Witch* promises to be one of those volumes that you will return to time and again."
—Andrew Theitic, publisher of *The Witches' Almanac*

"A text which I believe should become the go-to book on the subject for decades to come!"
—Sorita d'Este, author of *Practical Elemental Magick*

"Mat's work is helpful, practical, gentle, and supportive…It's a must-have for every witch's bookshelf."
—Courtney Weber, author of *The Morrigan*

"This book is chock-full of effective exercises and interesting perspectives."
—Anaar Niino, grandmaster of the Feri Tradition of Witchcraft and author of *The White Wand*

"Mat Auryn leads the reader through a well-thought-out series of practices …grounded in personal growth, mental health, and spiritual awareness."
—Diotima Mantineia, author of *Touch the Earth, Kiss the Sky*

"This is the foundational book on magical psychic development you didn't know you needed."
—Storm Faerywolf, author of *Forbidden Mysteries of Faery Witchcraft*

"There is no one more qualified or better prepared to write about witchcraft and psychic development than Mat Auryn."
—Jason Mankey, author of *Transformative Witchcraft*

"*Psychic Witch* is a feast of information presented clearly and with incredible detail—a master class on making the most of your innate psychic ability."
—Deborah Blake, author of *Everyday Witchcraft*

"*Psychic Witch* walks us through a process developing all the many rich ways in which humans sense the Otherworld."
—Lee Morgan, author of *Sounds of Infinity*

"An excellent and accessible piece of work, and I recommend it highly to anyone looking to deepen their psychic abilities."
—Aidan Wachter, author of *Six Ways: Approaches & Entries for Practical Magic*

"Mat Auryn puts a lot of magical theory in one place and explains it with a clear simplicity."
—Robin Artisson, author of *An Carow Gwyn: Sorcery and the Ancient Fayerie Faith*

"*Psychic Witch* answers so many questions to the magical practitioner who has opened up their psychic centers."
—Jacki Smith, author of *Coventry Magic*

"I believe Mat's perspective is critically important to the next generation of witches…I wish I'd had this book twenty years ago!"
—Thorn Mooney, author of *Traditional Wicca*

"*Psychic Witch* is an amazingly comprehensive exploration into the psychic arts."
—Laura Tempest Zakroff, author of *Sigil Witchery*

"Mat Auryn draws upon deep insight and years of experience to present the reader with an immensely practical guide."
—Gemma Gary, author of *Traditional Witchcraft*

psychic
WITCH

About the Author

Mat Auryn is a witch, professional psychic, and occult teacher based in New England. He has been drawn to the occult and metaphysical since an early age, reading books on witchcraft at eight years old. He is an initiate of Black Rose Witchcraft, the Cabot Tradition of Witchcraft, and the Temple of Witchcraft. He is currently a high priest in the Sacred Fires Tradition of Witchcraft. Mat has had the honor and privilege of studying under Christopher Penczak, Laurie Cabot, Devin Hunter, Storm Faerywolf, Chas Bogan, Jason Miller, and other prominent witchcraft teachers and elders.

He runs the blog *For Puck's Sake* on Patheos Pagan, is a content creator for *Modern Witch*, writes a column in *Witches & Pagans* magazine entitled Extrasensory Witchcraft, and writes a column in *Horns* magazine. He has been featured in various magazines, radio shows, podcasts, books, anthologies, and other periodicals. Mat was the very first recipient of the "Most Supportive Witch Award" presented by *Witch Way* magazine for helping others in the witchcraft community and going above and beyond to make other witches feel like they are not alone.

Mat has had the honor of helping thousands of people throughout the world gain clarity through his skills of psychic ability and tarot reading over the last decade. Mat teaches various metaphysical and occult subjects such as psychic development, magickal empowerment, working with spirits, divination, energy healing, lucid dreaming, divination, and astral projection.

To find out more about him and his work visit www.MatAuryn.com.

psychic
WITCH

A Metaphysical
Guide to
Meditation,
Magick &
Manifestation

MAT AURYN

Llewellyn Publications
Woodbury, Minnesota

FIRST EDITION
Fourteenth Printing, 2023

Book design by Samantha Penn
Cover design by Kevin Brown
Cover illustration and interior illustrations on pages 39, 42, 45, 57, 86, 88, 108, 140, 142, 143 and 181 by Tim Foley; remainder of illustrations by Llewellyn Art Department
Editing by Holly Vanderhaar

Llewellyn Publications is a registered trademark of Llewellyn Worldwide Ltd.

Library of Congress Cataloging-in-Publication Data
Names: Auryn, Mat, author.
Title: Psychic witch : a metaphysical guide to meditation, magick &
    manifestation / Mat Auryn.
Description: First edition. | Woodbury, Minnesota : Llewellyn Publications,
    2020. | Includes bibliographical references and index.
Identifiers: LCCN 2019044350 (print) | LCCN 2019044351 (ebook) | ISBN
    9780738760841 (paperback) | ISBN 9780738760865 (ebook)
Subjects: LCSH: Magic. | Psychic ability. | Witchcraft.
Classification: LCC BF1611 .A825 2020 (print) | LCC BF1611 (ebook) | DDC
    133.4/3—dc23
LC record available at https://lccn.loc.gov/2019044350
LC ebook record available at https://lccn.loc.gov/2019044351

Llewellyn Worldwide Ltd. does not participate in, endorse, or have any authority or responsibility concerning private business transactions between our authors and the public.

All mail addressed to the author is forwarded but the publisher cannot, unless specifically instructed by the author, give out an address or phone number.

Any internet references contained in this work are current at publication time, but the publisher cannot guarantee that a specific location will continue to be maintained. Please refer to the publisher's website for links to authors' websites and other sources.

Llewellyn Publications
A Division of Llewellyn Worldwide Ltd.
2143 Wooddale Drive
Woodbury, MN 55125-2989
www.llewellyn.com

Printed in China

In Memory of Raven Grimassi
(1951–2019)

"If the art of Witchcraft can be reduced to one aspect, it would be the achieving of altered states of consciousness…On a deeper level, we can add trance (induced by whatever means) and psychic development. Such states of consciousness allow the Witch not only to perceive things behind their veneer but also to reshape reality in an experiential sense."

—Raven Grimassi
The Witches' Craft: The Roots of Witchcraft & Magical Transformation

DEDICATION

This book is dedicated to the four largest influences on my magickal path, in chronological order: Silver RavenWolf, Christopher Penczak, Laurie Cabot, and Devin Hunter.

Silver, your work opened up a world of possibilities when it came to magick and witchery for me as a child. Your work alone was a gateway that jump-started my path of spirituality. Most of all, I learned not to limit my dreams based on what seemed "realistic." As a child, I would tirelessly (and sometimes obsessively) copy the information from your books with that little crescent moon on the spine into my own notebooks and eventually my first personal Book of Shadows. I dreamed of someday writing and publishing my own book with that Llewellyn logo on it, and here I am with my own, having achieved what seemed unrealistic. Thank you for the monumental impact that your work has had on my generation of budding witches and those before and after me.

Christopher, you reawakened my passion for witchcraft and psychic ability, and your work has brought it to the next level for me. In many ways, this book is my love letter to *The Inner Temple of Witchcraft*, a book that completely changed my personal practice in profound ways. Despite being a living occult encyclopedia, you're able to take very complex topics and break them down in an easy-to-understand manner to ensure your readers and students understand the concepts. Your ability to stay humble and grounded are qualities that I'm continually striving for. You have been a spiritual role model, a mentor, a friend, and an older brother, and I am a better person and a better witch because of it. The friendship and guidance that you provided during the writing of this book is priceless. Xoxotl forever!

Laurie, this book wouldn't exist without your pioneering work to combine psychic ability and witchcraft together. In my eyes, there is no one else who exemplifies the psychic witch more than you. It has been a great honor to take classes with you and to chat with you between readings at Enchanted. You predicted that this book would exist, and as always, you were right! Thank you for all the work you've done to educate the world about what witchcraft truly is, and for not only setting an example that psychic ability and magick are real, but for having people prove it to themselves in your classes.

Devin, when it comes to magick and witchcraft, I'm not sure I've ever seen eye-to-eye with anyone as much as I do with you. I definitely believe we're cut from the same cloth. You have invested outrageous amounts of time and energy into my training. You never gave up on me, you took the time to ask me questions and check in on me when I was off, you've called me on my crap, you've motivated me, you've encouraged me, you've tested me, you've held up mirrors, you've supported me, you've pushed me to grow, you've challenged me, you've inspired me, and you've also known when to give me space, when to trust my own capability, and most of all you never stopped believing in me or my potential. Many friends and acquaintances have commented that I'm an entirely different person inside and out and that I've grown and shifted immensely in positive ways as a person since I've started training with you. If that is true, a majority of that is solely due to your mentoring. I am extremely honored to have you as a friend, mentor, and co-conspirator.

CONTENTS

❧ EXERCISES ❧

Chapter 4

Chapter 5

Chapter 6

ILLUSTRATIONS

Chapter 14

CONSECRATION

This book is consecrated in the name of He who sees the past, present, and future with perfect clarity, who holds the key to time, and wears the lemniscate crown.

This book is consecrated in the name of She of the crossroads, mistress of all arcane arts, who holds the keys to all worlds, and wears the ouroboric crown.

Hail to the great psychic and the great witch.

OTHER ACKNOWLEDGMENTS

First and foremost, I would like to acknowledge Rory McCracken, without whom this book would have not been possible. Beyond those in the dedication, I also want to acknowledge everyone who has helped, encouraged, or inspired me to get to this point:

Adam Sartwell, Aidan Wachter, Ali Dossary, Alura Rose, Amy Blackthorn, Anaar Niino, Andrew Theitic, Anne Niven, Beth Beauregard, Brandon Blair, Brandon Smith and the Anix, Chas Bogan, Chester Sesco, Chris LeVasseur, Chris Morris, Chris Orapello, Courtney Weber, Cyndi Brannen, Danielle Dulsky, Danielle Dionne, Daniel Schulke, David Erwin, David Salisbury, Deborah Blake, Diotima Mantineia, Durgadas Allon Duriel, Elizabeth Autumnalis, Elysia Gallo, F. Steven Isom, Gemma Gary, Gwion Raven, Holly Vanderhaar, Irma Kaye Sawyer, Ivo Dominguez Jr., Jackie Smith, Jason Mankey, Jason Miller, Jess Carlson, Jim Shackleford, Judika Illes, Kat Sanborn, Kit Yarber, Laura Tempest Zakroff, Lauryn Heineman, Lee Morgan, Lonnie Scott, Madame Pamita, Matthew Venus, Michelle Belanger, Maxine Sanders, Mickie Mueller, Mike Blair, Nicholas Pearson, Oceana Leblanc, Penny Cabot, Phoenix LeFae, Raven Grimassi, Robbi Packard, Robin Artisson, Sarah Lynne Bowman, Sharon Day, Sorita d'Este, Stephanie Taylor, Steve Kenson, Storm Faerywolf, Sylvie Dugas, Tara Love-Maguire, Tess Whitehurst, Thorn Mooney, Tiffany Nicole Ware, Enchanted of Salem, the Robin's Nest, Moth and Moon Studio, the Mystic Dream, *Modern Witch*, the Temple of Witchcraft, the Sacred Fires Tradition of Witchcraft, Black Rose Witchcraft, the Cabot Tradition of Witchcraft, Coven of the Crown, the Black Flame Council, Patheos Pagan, and of course Llewellyn Worldwide.

FOREWORD

*"Our third-eye lets us see energy, if we are open
to it. For most people this is a foreign concept, but
once you let go of your prejudices and self-imposed
limitations, you will open to this talent."*
—Christopher Penczak, *Spirit Allies*

Embracing your power and path as a psychic being can be the most rewarding experience a witch can have in their lifetime. When we finally suspend our disbelief long enough to hold close the simple truth that to be a witch is to be psychic incredible things start to happen. Throughout the darker points in history, wielding such gifts as mediumship, prophecy, aura reading, and even vivid dreaming would likely lead others to consider you a witch.

Being psychic is not as glamorous as we are led to believe from watching television and reading blogs, though. Simply having the gift doesn't mean you can do anything useful with it, and knowing where to begin the process of developing that gift into something meaningful can be a daunting task—so daunting that many never even scratch the surface of what they are capable of becoming. Like many others, I found myself exploring witchcraft and the occult as a means of understanding my natural gifts, but there wasn't much information to find. Witches were always described as, and expected to be, these mystical figures with uncanny psychic ability, but I wasn't necessarily finding that to be true once I was on the inside.

I discovered that just because witches were expected to be psychic, that didn't mean that they were naturally gifted at being psychic. What's more, teaching someone how to use their natural abilities, when present, was a difficult task at best. The majority of people writing on the subject developed the ability to be psychically sensitive through their studies in the occult. Those who did have a deeper level of understanding often did not identify as witches and did everything they could do to separate themselves from the label. As Paganism and the occult began to reemerge onto the spiritual scene, there was a great importing of ideas, philosophies, and practices from groups and cultures that had already embraced the psychic. This went a long way in helping us piece together practices that could be applied to our work in the Craft, but still remained something separate from it, and if you wanted to go deep with the practices of psychic development, you still needed to look outside of the Craft for help.

It has only been in recent history that this has started to change, as authors like Laurie Cabot, Silver RavenWolf, and Christopher Penczak (to name a few) have leaned in on the conversation and have helped to bridge the gap between psychic development and modern witchcraft. What we have learned from their work and that of their contemporaries is that these two worlds weren't always separate and, in reality, they quite naturally fit together. Psychic ability is something inherent in every witch; it merely needs to be nurtured. Like most skills, it is something that witches have the ability to do, it's just that some of us have a knack for it, while others struggle to find their compass.

In this book, Mat Auryn continues this conversation with the goal of helping us find that compass, no matter our skill level or natural predilections. He puts his years as a professional psychic and witch to use and takes on the challenge of laying out a digestible yet detailed exploration of psychism as it relates to witchcraft, and he succeeds beautifully. What we find in this book is a well-researched and intimate look at tying the pieces together to not only sharpen our senses, but to enrich our magick as well.

Those approaching the subject for the first time will find a rich repository of practices and knowledge that will help to awaken dormant psychic abilities and put them to good use in their craft. This isn't apparent just in his attention to detail, but in the slivers of gnosis that Mat wraps up in every topic. We the readers are treated to an intimate look at a fundamental praxis that could only come from years of personal development and experimentation.

Those who are naturally gifted or who are taking their practice to the next level will find that Mat's own natural abilities as a psychic have given him unique insight: insight that proves to be informative and inspiring time and time again.

What sticks out most in this book is the emphasis on fusing the landscape of psychic development and witchcraft into a single practice. As I mentioned earlier, when I began my studies books like this did not exist. We had to go outside of witchcraft to find our answers. Here, we are finally given a manual on how to have an authentic witchcraft practice that includes psychic ability as a basic component.

Mat is part of a new generation of witches who continue to carry the torch of spiritual development into the twenty-first century, bridging the old-school and the new. Some will see his use of terms like brainwave entrainment, the Shadow Self, synchronicity, and reality mapping as too New Age. Others might find subjects like the Three Souls, quintessence, True Will, and the Witch Fire to be too dark and witchy. In the past, these were things that would remain separate from one another, but here they are woven together to create a tapestry of practices that have the potential to truly change your craft, no matter where you are starting from. These things are not presented to add fluff or to make our author sound smart; they are there to hold together the fundamental aspects of embracing our potential and taking our witchcraft to a whole new level.

In his professional life, Mat has spent years working with the public and helping seekers like you and me find the answers we were looking for. Sometimes this comes in the form of a reading, sometimes a class or a blog, but Mat's love of service and commitment to helping others is always present. As a student within Sacred Fires, he has surpassed my wildest expectations as his mentor, and I find myself in awe of his work and his continual progress. He is always moving forward, always ready to get his hands dirty and tackle difficult subjects—all while being there for his fellow students and tradition-mates as they do the same. He is the genuine deal; a real psychic witch who has built a life on being helpful to those in need.

In this book you will not find a bunch of spells to fix your problems; I think the title probably gave that away. What you will find, however, are tools that will help you to unlock your potential as a witch. Our problems in life are usually tied to that very thing: not living up to our potential. It isn't easy; it is actually some of the most difficult work we can do, but Mat knows this and takes us where we need to go with perfect love and perfect trust in our ability to succeed where we may not have before.

With the mind of a scholar and the heart of a coach, Mat provides us with a new take on often complex and complicated subjects and gives us the keys to unlocking their power within. Rooted in the old mysteries, flavored with the new, *Psychic Witch* is the book I wish I had had all those years ago; it skillfully continues the discussion of psychism in the Craft like no other book before.

Devin Hunter
Author of the Witch Power series
Founder of the Sacred Fires Tradition of Witchcraft

INTRODUCTION

For many people, the words *psychic* and *witch* are seen as words reserved for fiction. The words may conjure up ideas from movies and television such as *American Horror Story*, *Salem*, *The Craft*, *Chilling Adventures of Sabrina*, or perhaps the witches of *Hocus Pocus*, or maybe even fraudulent scam artists pretending to be psychic. Though it is not my intention to prove that both psychic ability and magickal ability are real on blind faith alone, let me assure you that they are. My goal is not for you to just take my word for it, but to have you prove this to yourself through direct experience by the time you come to the end of this book.

Psychic and Magickal Power Is Our Birthright

In both psychic and magickal circles, there's quite a bit of gatekeeping. This is unfortunate. Gatekeeping is best defined as an attempt to control and limit who can be a part of a certain group or activity. There's a strong notion that you can only be born with magickal or psychic aptitude. While you definitely can be born with a predisposition to these realms, just as one might be born with a predisposition to art or athletics, it is definitely not the only way to attain them. In fact, it often becomes a form of lazy elitism to make such statements. Just as with art or sports, continual training, dedication, and practice are necessary for development and maintenance.

I once had a client in a psychic reading who kept referring to my "gift," saying that I was the one with a gift that they claimed they did not have. I kept reassuring them that it's not necessarily a gift, but an ability that must be developed and continuously worked at to help maintain and strengthen it. This client didn't seem to believe me at first but I reassured her that it was absolutely true. I invited her to one of my psychic development workshops in which I taught psychic techniques, many of which I am sharing in this book. I had her prove to herself that anyone, even she, could be psychic. This excited her greatly and put her on a quest to learn more and more, and to keep working at it. She is now a professional psychic reader a few years later.

Some folks will say that these are things that must be passed down genetically in the family or that only certain groups, cultures, ethnicities, or genders can possess these abilities. This is absolutely incorrect. Not only do we see magick and psychic ability universally throughout history in both genders, but as humans, we all share a common ancestry—one that if you trace it far back enough is pagan and magickal. So let me make this crystal clear: anyone can perform magick and everyone is psychic. Magick and psychic ability aren't supernatural but rather completely natural and absolutely possible for every single human being to engage in. We were born to embrace our full potential, to use all of our abilities, and to experience and interact with the world around us to the fullest degree possible.

Combining Psychic Power and Witchcraft

Both *psychic* and *witch* are heavily charged words, so much so that many people who are psychics or witches try to dodge the words altogether. They may find other words to be more comfortable and accepted by outsiders—words such as *intuitive, empath, Pagan,* or *energy worker.* However, one of the problems that I often find is that through the toning down of these labels and attempts to make them more palatable to the general public, there's often a lessening of the full potential of psychic and magickal ability as well. The succinctness of thoughts, emotions, and words only enhances the psychic and the magickal—and the words *psychic* and *witch* are two very succinct words that evoke very strong thoughts and emotions. To me, these words conjure up a level of adeptness and power within their respective realms. Lowering the bar of these practices serves no one.

Magick ability and psychic perception may seem like two completely different things at first. Just as the Roman god Janus is depicted with two faces on a singular being, the psychic and magickal are two sides of one coin. At the core, they're aspects of how we are engaging and interacting with subtle energies. Psychic ability is also commonly referred to as extrasensory perception, wherein one is able to perceive energy as information through various means.

Folk etymologies have their place in our collective psyche and are often used among magickal teachers. The word *witch* is often connected to the word *Wicca*, which is popularly passed on by elders of the Craft as meaning "to bend," "shape," or "wield." While there's not really a lot of strong evidence of this being a historical etymological definition, it's an effective idea that gets to the heart of what witchcraft is when you strip all the different trappings and traditions away. In other words, the Craft of witchery revolves around "the ability to manipulate energy and shape it for desired outcomes."

Many witches rush through their basics and their daily practice. Perhaps this is because they're entirely focused on completing tasks for a level of training that they're going through and moving on to the next stage. Maybe it's because they are not taking personal accountability for their practice and growth and are relying instead on the validation of their teacher to tell them that they've mastered a particular stage. Perhaps they've become bored with the work that they're doing. Maybe they assume that something more complex means that it's more powerful and they therefore are seeking the powerful.

Just because something is basic or simple does not mean that it isn't immensely powerful. Magick changes everyone that it touches and everyone who touches magick changes. It's important to understand that all initiations are beginnings and not endings. I have found continual unfolding of attunement and depth in the basic practices that many others may set aside as being part of their past practice as beginners.

There are times when magickal practitioners can lose their love for magick despite engaging in complex rituals and magickal practices. I've had many witches tell me that their magick was no longer working and that they were getting bored with the Craft. This may lead them down other avenues of exploration in regard to spirituality, but in my experience is usually a call to revisit the basics. It is within the basics that we can find new depth. I have seen dedicated and earnest seekers begin to radiate energetically just from grounding and centering themselves.

Whatever you touch will touch you back. The simplest way that I can try to explain it is that when you spend time touching the core of the earth, soaking in the stars, communing with the moon, aligning with the elements, working with the gods and spirits—it changes a person. It's as if their wavelength begins synchronizing to different wavelengths and the person's energy hums like a symphony. Sometimes we feel this through psychic means, but often we experience it as just an intensely strong comfort with the individual, a sense of familiarity and kinship, and a high level of respect, even if we don't recognize exactly why. There's just this knowing in regard to the nature of their heart and spirit. I believe this is because we're feeling the energies within them that we spend so much time with ourselves, so there's this recognition. You can feel the energies that they've spent time with because you've spent time with those energies as well. There's just this je ne sais quoi about them.

Witchcraft is often considered a crooked path that weaves serpentine between the right-hand and left-hand paths. I am not convinced that this path has a destination, but rather that the path itself is about the journey. I suspect that this serpentine path is ouroboric, having no true beginning or end.

I'm Here to Help

As a practicing witch who is very active in both my local community and the greater online community—and through my experience as a professional psychic interacting with other psychics—I have noticed something. There are a lot of witches that are not that great when it comes to psychic abilities; there are also a lot of talented psychics who are absolutely blocked when it comes to magick and manifestation. I have met so many witches who are completely unsure if the spirits and gods that they're working with are even there, or are unsure if they've cast a circle or raised energy other than the simple fact that they followed directions. It's like they're working completely blind. I have also met psychics who can give other people fantastic life advice and clarity but struggle to pay their rent, remove obstacles, and manifest opportunities.

This is by no means a judgment; rather, it's something that I understand from my own experience as well. There were many early years when I would try casting spells, and they just wouldn't work. I would follow the instructions, have the right ingredients, and recite all the words—yet it would still fall short of manifesting any sort of concrete outcome. Magick isn't about empty rituals, words, or objects. The key to magick is the manipulation of energy, and energy is best worked with when it can be perceived.

Through the years of my deep immersion within both the psychic and magickal worlds, I began seeing how these two abilities not only work together but also how greatly they complement and strengthen one another. You can use magick to enhance your psychic ability, and you can use psychic ability to enhance your magick. I have sought out some of the most prominent and well-respected teachers of magick and psychic ability to study with through the years, and this has only strengthened my conclusion that they're not merely intertwined—they are two halves of one whole.

Through the experience of my own practice, and through years of actively teaching others both psychic and magickal development, I have been able to boil down the foundations of awakening to your psychic senses and wielding energy. I have left room for experimentation and adaptability. There are absolutely no one-size-fits-all methods for perceiving and working with energy. Individuals are individuals, and we're all wired differently—thus, different things work for different folks. I have kept this in mind throughout the book and will help you to explore your own relationship to these methods. I have also stripped away techniques and trappings that are specific to certain traditions of witchcraft as much as possible. What is left are core ideas and components that are similar throughout the various traditions I have trained in, and among teachers of other traditions that I've read and spoken with, such as the Three Souls and the Three World models.

Through my own experimentation, I have found that there are ways around certain culturally specific practices without appropriating them as our own, simply by using a cosmological system that is a bit more universal in nature. While the Divine is touched upon, I have left room for you to modify this based on your own spiritual beliefs and have also provided some angles to work through this for those who are more atheistic in their approach to witchcraft or psychic ability. I have approached the subject of the Divine through the vague term of *Spirit*, which is open to personal interpretation such as *the Divine Mind*, *the Universe*, *Source*, *God*, *Goddess*, or *the*

Star Goddess—even if your interpretation is that it's a psychological tool to access something deeper within you.

You may also notice that there are few to no tools or materials necessary for the work in this book aside from your mind, body, and spirit; it lacks the pomp and circumstance of what is viewed as a traditional spell. That is intentional; I want the reader to understand and master the energies that they're working with before they venture into proper spellwork. Mastering the perception and manipulation of energy is crucial before you move forward to effective spellcasting. However, you will be amazed at what you can do with only your mind, body, and spirit.

My aim is not to assist you in becoming merely a powerful psychic or a powerful witch, but to make you a powerful psychic witch. To me, a psychic witch is one who not only perceives information with all of their inner and outer senses in all of the realms of reality but one who is also able to directly experience, interact with, and manipulate them for their own advantage. Throughout this book, I will be sharing some of my most closely guarded tips, secrets, practices, and meditations. While it may be tempting to skip around to sections that seem interesting to you, I strongly advise viewing this as a course in which all elements build upon one another. You'll also be given exercises along with a model of the soul, a model of different planes of existence, and concepts related to divinity. Regardless of what your personal beliefs are surrounding these topics, I encourage you to approach this book as if the concepts are true, as they're serving a purpose and building toward something else.

I encourage you to learn the rules, cosmology, and praxis as laid out here before modifying them to reflect your own tradition or spiritual path. Due to the spiritual and metaphysical nature of these topics, it's hard to say with any certainty that this is the way that things are. But I can say with certainty that following the concepts as if they are true will yield great results. At the least, view it as a giant thought experiment of holding it to be true for the purposes of this book. Learn the rules first and break them when you've thoroughly experienced and understood them as I'm teaching them.

I believe that different people get different things out of witchcraft and spirituality. But for those with a focus on mastering magick, witchcraft takes work. It takes dedication. It takes perseverance. For some, these statements will stir up insecurities of inadequacy, and that isn't my intention. My intention here is to hopefully inspire and motivate you in your practice.

Though I teach and share, I see myself as a seeker and a student first and foremost. I sincerely believe that an earnest beginner witch lighting a candle for the first time and making a simple wish with a focused will can be infinitely more powerful than a seasoned witch who is performing a complicated rite from an archaic book of magick for the same goal, if that seasoned witch is just going through the motions without sincerity. It all depends on the level of work that they've put into their path and practice and how much of their heart is in it.

From where I am in my path it appears to me that mastery is not so much about reaching a specific end goal, but instead about seeing how deep you can take practice and striving to better your experience with it. Meditation, for example, is one of the most straightforward techniques out there—but it is also one of the most profound and transformative. The simple act of closing your eyes, focusing on nothing but your breath, can seem basic and easily tempting to rush through. But how many people do you know who cannot meditate, who cannot clear their minds or focus on solely one thing with every sense engaged with it?

You can't build a magnificent structure on a weak foundation and expect it to stand the test of time. Regardless of where you are on your path, ensure that part of your daily spiritual and magickal routine involves deepening into the basics. How much deeper can a simple practice element of magick go? I encourage you not to lose sight of the foundations. We *practice* witchcraft—perhaps because it is something that can never truly be mastered, but rather something that we deepen and strive to perfect just a little better every time we engage in it.

This book is written for everyone regardless of experience level and is meant to be an entry point for some. While some of the fundamental practices and concepts may seem basic to more seasoned practitioners, I encourage you to revisit them with me. Being adept in these fields isn't about how complex you build upon the foundation, but how much richness you can gain in your practices by diving into the core elements. You may discover a new level of depth by returning to them. It is my hope that this book will present these practices and ideas in a new light that both the novice seeker and the most seasoned practitioner can sink their teeth into.

Chapter 1
THE POWER AND THE SIGHT

Witchcraft and psychic ability are natural human traits that we as a species have slowly lost touch with in the post-industrial age. Witchcraft is known by countless names. Depending on the culture and period, the terms may be different and may carry different connotations, but the heart is the same. In older times, the witch was the one who had what was known as "the power," or what we call today the ability to use magick. The psychic, on the other hand, was one who had "the sight" or "second sight," the ability to see and sense beyond the five physical senses.

But what exactly is witchcraft? Witchcraft is an umbrella term for many different practices, and the definition of a witch may vary from person to person. I have come to think of witchcraft as being as unique and diverse as the individual soul of the person, since the way each person relates to and interacts with unseen spiritual forces is going to be unique to them. Witchcraft and psychic ability are not just merely practices or crafts. They are a state of being and an orientation. In other words, it's how we orient ourselves with our environment, both seen and unseen reality. The psychic and the witch are both occultists. "The occult" means that which is hidden, just as the moon eclipsing the sun hides the sunlight. The occultist studies and interacts with these hidden truths, peering beyond the veil of perception. They understand that there is a metaphysical reality that transcends our ordinary senses of physical reality.

As an orientation, some may be born with a more natural disposition to experience and interact with the metaphysical, just as some people are born with more of a predisposition to athletic or artistic skill and talent than others. This is not to say that only those who are born with that innate openness can be witches or psychics, but rather that it is an orientation. Orientation is a position or perspective of someone relative to something else. This means that one can reorient oneself toward the metaphysical through study, practice, work, and experience.

One who may not have been as naturally predisposed to the occult has the potential to surpass those who do have this orientation yet never work at enhancing it. You don't have to have been born a certain way or have any natural talent to become a talented psychic or witch. You just need earnest effort and dedication. It is also my belief that some witches are so good at the occult that they've obscured the fact that they're natural witches from even themselves. Some of the most powerful witches I have ever met would be horrified at being called a witch.

The experience of the metaphysical is perceived through the *clairs*. The clairs, meaning "clear" in French, have a more precise perception and experience of the five ordinary senses that extends beyond their usual limitations. In other words, the clairs are often defined as extrasensory perception. With extrasensory perception, sight becomes clairvoyance, touch becomes clairtangency, taste becomes clairgustance, hearing becomes clairaudience, and smell becomes clairalience. Among the clairs, one may also have clairempathy (psychic emotional experiences), clairsentience (psychic physical sensations within the body), and claircognizance (psychic knowing).

Despite this, I have come to believe that extrasensory perception isn't necessarily our senses extended beyond our physical or ordinary senses—though that's how it's defined and an easy way to explain it. Rather, I have come to believe that our psychic senses are our primary senses, the senses we have as spirit beings, and our physical senses are extensions of those primary psychic senses. We come into this world and into the womb with our psychic senses fully developed; it's only after birth, as a child develops and ages, that these psychic senses recede while our physical senses take over. As physical beings, our physical senses are limited to as far as one can touch, hear, taste, smell, and so on. But as spiritual beings, which we are before and after physical incarnation, our psychic senses are limitless.

The terms *psychic ability* and *intuition* are often used interchangeably and are related concepts, but I distinguish between the two. Intuition is the unconscious processing of sensory information in one's environment to come to a particular conclusion. Psychic ability, on the other hand, is the processing of extrasensory perception that doesn't rely on primary sensory information about one's environment. Intuition feels more natural and ordinary to most people and usually falls into the claircognizance category of just knowing or the clairempathy category of feeling a certain way about something without knowing why one does.

In other words, intuition is based on perceivable external environmental information, whereas psychic ability is not. The two often work synchronistically together, and by becoming more in tune with your intuition, you will become a stronger psychic as you learn to listen to yourself and notice how you perceive information. I view intuition as the Middle Self processing information from the Lower Self, and psychic ability as the Middle Self processing information from the Higher Self. These are concepts which we'll dive into more thoroughly later.

At all times, subtle hidden forces are affecting our lives. We may be aware of this and interact with them. We may also be completely unaware and still interact with them. The ability to interact and manipulate energy without perceiving it is what occult author and teacher Ivo Dominguez Jr. calls "a noir perception," *noir* being the French word for dark. It's an inability to clearly perceive the energy being manipulated on a conscious psychic level, but an ability to manage the energy still.[1] Many modern witches fall under this category. They may conduct a whole spell or ritual without ever perceiving any of the energy that is moving around during their casting. Likewise, many psychics may perceive energies but cannot consciously interact or alter them.

The psychic witch, however, has a direct perception and interaction with the concealed forces of reality. The psychic witch communes with the spirits, the rocks, the streams, the stars, and the wind. They come to see and understand the underlying hidden programs and processes that compose the Universe. They observe the patterns and begin to understand the laws of cause

---

1. Ivo Dominguez Jr., *The Keys To Perception: A Practical Guide to Psychic Development* (Newburyport, MA: Weiser Books, 2017), 49–53.

and effect, being able to see the unfolding of one part of life and trace the chain back to the source cause. They can look at the things being put into motion at the moment and predict how they will play out in the future.

The psychic witch lives in a state of enchantment, seeing all things as magickal and understanding that the Universe is composed of endless possibilities and potential. The psychic witch sees a door where others see a wall. Recognizing that all things are connected and related to one another, the psychic witch knows how to put energies into action to achieve a particular outcome consciously. This is magick. Magick is the manipulation of subtle energies in a specific manner to influence a desired result. It is through altering consciousness and harnessing one's willpower that the psychic witch can cast magick purposefully and with precision.

Reality Is Energy

Reality is composed entirely of energy. Mystics, psychics, witches, and other practitioners of magick have always known this truth. This isn't just a mystical perspective—it's also the nature of physics. Everything that seems solid is merely energy vibrating at a slower rate; when we examine it on microscopic levels we find that solid matter is made of particles perpetually in motion. Even this book you're holding is just energy. Everything we can touch, hear, see, taste, and smell is simply energy in different forms being perceived by our senses, but energy is not limited to what we can measure with our senses.

There's energy that exceeds our normal five senses. Those who are more skeptical will often say things such as "seeing is believing" or may scoff at the idea of unseen energy. Yet it only takes a quick look around us to understand that we cannot perceive or see all the energy around us. Magnetic fields and radiation are examples of energies that we're constantly interacting with that are invisible to our eyes, as are wireless signals and ultraviolet light.

Our perception also differs from that of other animals, who experience reality on different levels. Animals perceive energetic information that would seem supernatural if a human were to naturally sense it in the same way. There are animals and insects that can perceive a much broader spectrum of light and color than humans. There are also frequencies of sound (which is an energy, too) inaudible to human beings that other animals can hear. While we can hear a wide spectrum of sound waves, we cannot hear them all.

The noise coming from a dog whistle is energy that our bodies are not equipped to perceive, yet dogs most definitely hear it. There's also a bombardment of radio waves that we're interacting with that cannot be heard without using a device to tune into that specific frequency. Seemingly psychic to the human, dogs can be trained to smell cancer on someone. There are even energies that are experienced completely differently by some animals. Dolphins and bats can use sound through echolocation and experience it as a form of sight. Migratory birds have a perception of the magnetic field and about the weather that informs their migration and that is still a bit of a mystery to scientists.

But why? Evolution has wired humans and animals to scan the environment for information that is vital for survival. In other words, we have evolved so that our perception is directly related to what we need to know to survive. Our senses as we perceive them are merely meant to help us survive daily existence so that our species can continue living in a physical reality. Forms of perception that are not considered important to survival in a species will be abandoned as evolution proceeds in favor of developing senses that do. Furthermore, we live in a society that has a strong focus on the "real world" with an emphasis on what can be perceived. This often leads to a suppression of any senses beyond the five physical ones, yet they aren't gone—they're still there.

Have you ever thought of someone you haven't communicated with in a long time and suddenly they called or texted you? Have you ever had a gut feeling about someone or a situation that turned out to be correct? Have you experienced déjà vu or had a dream that came to pass? Almost everybody has had moments when these other senses have suddenly opened, even if it's short-lived. We still have a whole system of perception that has only gone dormant in our species but is still there waiting to reawaken.

This also carries through when it comes to the psychic perception of subtle energy. Subtle energies are energies that aren't necessarily measurable or detectable to our senses or through science. We often have a hard time understanding a lot of the energy that we receive as information, simply because we're not programmed to understand it. We do not have a very precise way to describe energy as we perceive it, as our vocabulary for it is very underdeveloped. For example, until a child learns about the concept of *green* as a word, they may have a hard time discerning it from other colors. They also have a difficult time distinguishing colors that have similar hues. Once the child learns a larger vocabulary for the colors they see, they can not only name them but discern and differentiate "forest green" from "lime green." When it comes to energy perception, our words are not as accurate as they are for other senses we perceive until we learn a vocabulary for different energies.

This is true also for the perception of our senses like taste and smell, if you think about it. Think about how wine connoisseurs describe complex tastes such as wine. They'll use words like *earthy, fruity, buttery, toasty, flamboyant, sharp, oaky, charcoal, velvety,* and many others. This is because the mind can't find precise words in our language for what it's experiencing, so it tries to reference words that somehow describe the quality of what is on the palate as well as it can. We simply lack the language for it. Yet, to the average person, wine may not seem so complex. The same holds true for those who are musicians; they hear music differently because they understand the subtle changes of pitches, keys, harmonies, and melodies. Thus, they have an easier time talking about music since they have a vocabulary for it. The same is true with subtle energy. Learning to describe the qualities of different energies allows for precision. The precision of discerning and describing energies is what makes someone an effective psychic witch.

To the psychic witch, all subtle energy is a form of information. We receive energetic information that informs us about other people, events, situations, and our world around us. It allows us to have better judgment and ensure that we're on the right path. We can also conjure and manipulate energetic information and send it out into our world to actively affect those paths and their outcomes.

Brainwave States

So how do we begin perceiving energy beyond our five primary senses? Radios work by transmitting on different hertz frequencies. By tuning in to the right channel with the appropriate frequency on your radio, you are able to perceive that once unperceivable frequency. Like radio waves, our brains produce subtle electrical impulses generated by masses of neurons communicating to each other for particular activities that we are engaged in, and create specific states of consciousness. Each brainwave state is named after a Greek letter and is measured by the cycles per second called hertz. There are five brainwave states: gamma, beta, alpha, theta, and delta. Each one is distinguished by their hertz cycle, though there's area of overlap. By learning to alter our brainwave states we learn to alter our consciousness.

GAMMA—38–42 hertz: Once thought to be random brain noise, the mysterious gamma is the fastest brainwave state. Researchers have found that gamma is highly active when in universal love and transcendental states of consciousness associated with enlightenment. Some Tibetan Buddhist monks and some Indian yogis are able to display this brainwave state while meditating.

BETA—12–28 hertz: Beta occurs while we're awake, alert, and concentrating on something. This is the most common brainwave state that we engage in as humans. Excitement, anxiety, stress, decision-making, critical thinking, and focused attention are associated with beta.

ALPHA—7.5–13 hertz: Alpha occurs while we're relaxed, meditating, visualizing, and daydreaming. Alpha has access to the subconscious mind and occurs when we are receiving information passively, such as learning. Alpha is the state of consciousness that is most associated with psychic ability, and the state of consciousness linked with hypnosis.

THETA—4–7 hertz: Theta occurs before and after sleep. It is associated with light sleep, deep meditation, deep dreaming, vivid imagery, and high levels of inner awareness. In theta we become completely unaware of the external world.

DELTA—1–3 hertz: Delta occurs during periods of deep dreamless sleep and is associated with the deepest states of meditation. Healing and regenerating are associated with this state of consciousness, which is why deep sleep can be deeply healing.

As you can see, alpha and theta are the brainwave states that are associated with psychic perception. What is the main difference between these two? In alpha, you can still function. You can talk, you can walk, you can perform a ritual or spell, or you can give a tarot reading, whereas you can't (or at least effectively) while in theta, as you're beginning to fall asleep and beginning to lose an awareness of the external world as the inner realms of dreams begin to take over the perception of the external world.

To be a quality psychic you need to be able to reach a clear state somewhere between alpha and theta without falling asleep. Luckily, science has shown that all we need to do for our brain to begin generating alpha waves is to simply close our eyes for a small period and start visualizing. To reach theta all we need to do is begin visualizing and make those images within our Witch Eye much more vivid. It is in this state of mind that we get lost in daydream, replay memories in an immersive manner, as well as having access to unconscious images and perception.

The pineal gland is the Witch Eye and is referred to commonly as the *third eye* or the *mind's eye*. The pineal gland is about pea sized and is located in the middle of your head. If you place a finger on the top of your head right in the center and a finger on a spot above and between your eyebrows, where those two points meet is the location of the pineal gland. If you were to slice the human brain in half vertically between right and left hemispheres you would see that the pineal gland looks like an eye with glands surrounding it in a shape similar to the Egyptian Eye of Horus or Eye of Ra. Interestingly, the pineal gland itself looks a lot like a tiny eyeball.

While scientists aren't completely sure what the exact purpose of the pineal gland is in humans, we do know that in lower vertebrate animals that it acts in sync with their eyes as a sort of third eye, and contains light receptors and nerve cells, but this isn't the case in human beings where there are no light-sensitive receptors. However, we can see a link between the pineal gland, our eyes, and light, as we do know that the pineal gland sends neural signals for melatonin output and has a circadian rhythm associated with cycles of light and dark. Light is received by the eyes and sent to the brain via the optic nerve, which radiates to the nerves that supply the pineal gland. Darkness increases the output of norepinephrine, which is a neurotransmitter that releases melatonin, while light reduces the output.[2]

2. Jerry Vried and Nancy A. M. Alexiuk, "The Pineal Gland and Melatonin," in *Handbook of Endocrinology, Second Edition, Volume 1*, ed. George H. Gass and Harold M. Kaplan (Boca Raton, NY: CRC Press LLC, 1996), 7–8.

Melatonin is also fairly mysterious. Some researchers believe that there's a link between melatonin, sleep, and relaxation.[3] Many people who take melatonin as a supplement report much more vivid dreams as well. Here we see a possible link between light, the pineal gland, relaxation, and dreaming. Since both relaxation and brainwave states associated with daydreaming and light dreaming are important for psychic perception, you may start to realize that this is one of many reasons that witches and psychics tend to prefer to work in dimly lit spaces with candlelight in lieu of bright atmospheres. That's because there's more melatonin being produced, which may activate a more naturally relaxed state conducive to alpha, and the pineal gland is actively working.

Laurie Cabot, a world-renowned psychic and the Official Witch of Salem[4] believes that psychic perception occurs in the alpha state, because while you are in a trance state, your eyes begin to roll upward naturally toward the pineal gland.[5] She believes that all psychic information is unseen light and that the pineal gland receives this information and interprets it. When we're in alpha, there's a direct conversation going on between the conscious mind and the pineal gland.

Exercise 1

❧

Preliminary Focus

This is the first vital exercise to master before moving on. It may seem very simple at first, but you may find it's a bit more difficult than you expected. This is the ability to keep your mind entirely focused on one mental task. Affirm to yourself out loud or in your head that when you reach the number zero, you will be in the alpha brainwave state of consciousness. Proceed by counting down from the number one hundred to zero.

---

3. "Melatonin: In Depth," National Center for Complementary and Integrative Health, last modified July 16, 2018, https://nccih.nih.gov/health/melatonin.

4. An honorary title bestowed upon her in the 1970s by Governor Michael Dukakis of Massachusetts for her work in the community.

5. Laurie Cabot and Tom Cowan, *Power of the Witch: The Earth, the Moon, and the Magical Path to Enlightenment* (New York, NY: Delta, 1989), 175–177.

At this stage, it's unimportant whether you visualize the numbers in your Witch Eye or not. What is important is that the number you are on is the only thing that you are focused on at the moment. If you get distracted or realize that your mind has wandered, simply start over again. Once you have accomplished this successfully without any other thoughts invading, then see if you can achieve it three times in a row, stating your affirmation at the beginning each time. Once you have this down, you're ready to move on.

A Childlike Wonder

Children are often regarded as being more naturally psychic and magickal, and I would agree with this. In fact, there's a quote that's passed among several different traditions of witchcraft as a wisdom saying that is attributed to Lady Circe, a famous and influential witch, which states, "If you would walk the witch's way, observe with care the child at play." There indeed is wisdom and a key in this brief maxim.

There are a couple of factors that stick out to me about children and their predisposition to the psychic and magickal. The first is that children are fully engaged when they're having fun. The second is that their imaginations are in full swing. I believe this wise saying has a lot to do with those two factors. In fact, the most magickally talented people I know are fun people and mind-blowingly imaginative and creative. When children are having fun they're totally plugged in because they're engaged. Children seek out play, creativity, and fun.

Now think of a child that's not having fun. Think of a child who is completely bored. They're completely resistant even if that's not their intention. If you put a child in detention or sit them down for a boring class lecture, more often than not they will begin daydreaming. They're naturally wired to engage with their imagination. They are tuned into the alpha and theta brainwave states naturally, which are the same brainwave states that are activated when one begins daydreaming or engages their imagination.

Most of all, children essentially have a permission slip from society to be imaginative. Until about the age of seven years old they are predominantly in the alpha and theta brainwave states, meaning they are more prone to psychic experiences.[6] It is only as they grow older that imagination and creativity are condemned in favor of being practical, logical, and serious. It is then that these forms of perception begin to be suppressed and begin to go dormant waiting to be reawakened once again.

It is logical to conclude that this is the natural human state, as it's how children naturally are as they're being conditioned by external forces. Luckily, I have good news for you. You are a human and you were once a child. That means you already have the ability to reboot this part of your nature with a little bit of work, and I'm here to help you with this. We're going to start with a seemingly silly exercise of make-believe!

Exercise 2
Psychic Immersion

This is a very simple exercise, but you may surprise yourself with it. I want you to pick a day to pretend that you are an all-knowing and always accurate psychic. Conjure up examples of the all-knowing psychic archetype such as a mysterious fortune teller, or the witch who sees all and knows all.

It's important to not half-ass it. Really immerse yourself in the role just as a child would when playing make-believe with friends or alone to entertain themselves. Pretend you can see auras; what would those auras look like on different people? You don't have to actually know how to see auras yet, we're just pretending, so assign them a color based on how they're acting or who they are. The color doesn't need to match a list of aura color meanings. Make predictions throughout the day, and don't get discouraged if they end up being wrong; remember, this is just make-believe and you're make-believing that you're always right.

You can practice with a friend as well. In my workshops, I will have strangers partner up and they'll take turns pretending they're psychic and will proceed to just start making up a bunch of information about the person they're paired with. Who are they? What's their story? Where do they come from? What do they want out of life? What are their hopes and fears?

---

6. Ernst Niedermeyer and Fernando Lopes Da Silva, "Maturation of the EEG," in *Electroencephalography: Basic Principles, Clinical Applications, and Related Fields*, 5th ed. (Philedelphia, PA: Lippincott Williams & Wilkins, 1996), 225.

The key here is that the person being read can only confirm accurate statements and not tell them when they're wrong. The person being read will write down all the hits that they got correct. This is very important in any psychic development exercise that involves more than one person. Someone can be dead on the money and one piece of information may be off or wrong and as soon as they hear "no" the reader completely shuts down with doubt and no longer is able to convey accurate information because doubt has taken over.

This exercise is meant to give you permission to use your imagination and have fun outside of your normal comfort zones. It lifts the barriers of conditioning that suppress our ability to use these creative faculties and employ them in our daily lives. It also builds confidence, because it's extremely common that, while pretending, they will hit on a bunch of accurate information, especially the longer that they're in character and the deeper they go. However, accuracy is not the focus here. We will learn how to be accurate psychics as we proceed. But we first need to learn to crawl before we can run.

At the end of the day write your experience down. How did it feel to roleplay and immerse yourself into the character? Was it fun? Empowering? Uncomfortable? Could you feel societal programming creeping in, telling you that this was all nonsense? Were there any accurate hits? Was there anything that came to you that you're not able to verify yet?

Be honest in recording your thoughts, feelings, and experiences. Lying or holding back in your journal won't serve you. Part of the journaling experience is about seeing how you've grown through time and seeing what worked and what didn't work. Staying honest with how you truly feel and what you truly experienced is going to assist you in growing as a psychic witch.

Affirmations and Neuroplasticity

The power of affirmations is easily overlooked. Affirmations are simply positive statements about oneself, usually worded in the present tense and spoken out loud repeatedly for the purpose of programming yourself in a certain manner. As psychic witches, we understand the power of the spoken word and the power of thoughts. We understand that the internal world and external world are intricately linked. We know it's important that we take control of our own minds and energy so that we can step into our personal sovereignty.

Affirmations can change how you think. How? The brain is constantly creating and strengthening electro-chemical neural pathways that are used the most through constant stimulation. If a certain way of thinking is repeated, consciously or unconsciously, those pathways become the predominant ones used, leading to thinking or feeling in this manner more and more. This is called neuroplasticity. Now, energetically the same is true. Energy pathways that are used more become strengthened and easier to access, while those that are ignored become weakened. The energy body has its own form of memory.

A specific affirmation must be used daily and over prolonged periods of time. Those neuropathways and those energetic channels to those thought-forms aren't going to change overnight. Real change takes time and work. The most successful people I know and the most powerful witches I have met have all embraced affirmations. Affirmations have done wonders in my life and definitely shouldn't be overlooked.

Exercise 3

⚬≫⚬

Psychic Affirmations

Now it's your turn to do it. Every time you look in the mirror, stop and look yourself in the eyes. Affirm to yourself statements of your psychic prowess along with affirmations of self-love and self-empowerment. At that moment, believe every single thing that you're saying with all of your being. I could have you start by saying it daily for a week, or over a month, but honestly you should just incorporate affirmations into your daily life. Here are ten example affirmations that will help boost your psychic ability:

"I am psychic."
"I receive accurate information."
"I can feel and see subtle energy."
"My Witch Eye perceives with clarity."
"I can perceive the past, present, and future with accuracy."
"My psychic powers are growing every day."

"Psychic ability is easy and comes naturally for me."
"I receive guidance in my dreams and remember it."
"I trust my intuition."
"I am thankful for my ever-growing psychic gifts."

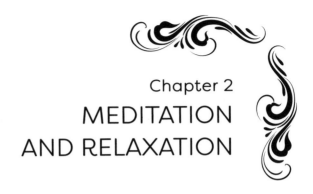

Chapter 2
MEDITATION
AND RELAXATION

Meditation is the foundation of all psychic ability and, in my personal opinion, all acts of magick. By investing in the practice of meditation, you are investing in your psychic and magickal ability. By learning to relax and by doing breath work we can quickly shift our brainwave state and level of consciousness, which puts us in an altered state that allows us to receive psychic information and perceive energies more readily. Why? Meditation teaches us about how our minds work, how to focus, and how to direct our awareness and therefore our will. Meditation is the greatest tool to enhancing your psychic ability and your magickal practice.

It's through meditation that we begin to know ourselves and our minds. Our minds are always filled with excess noise and imagery. Sometimes that noise and imagery is our creation, other times it's programming developed from a bombardment of information. By meditating, we learn how to silence our mind. Think of your mind as if it were a pond. If the pond is murky, we can't see anything beyond its surface. Through meditation, we clear this pond. When the pond is crystal clear, we can see both the bottom of the pond and anything that is reflecting upon the water's surface. We can then differentiate between what is being reflected in it and what is deep within it. The pond reflects without judgment or bias when completely clear. It is through this clarity that we can accurately begin receiving psychic impressions with the least amount of interference.

Meditation is a straightforward practice, but that doesn't mean that it's easy. I often hear people complaining about meditation or stating that they cannot do it. This is because meditation requires concentration, and genuinely concentrating on something with our full undivided attention can prove much more difficult than it sounds. The unfocused mind is often compared to a monkey, and in meditative practices, it is sometimes referred to as "monkey mind." Think of a monkey who cannot sit still and is swiftly moving through a jungle, swinging from one tree branch of thought to another tree branch. Through meditation, we learn to tame that monkey mind so that it can sit still and focus.

The biggest pitfalls in meditation involve making excuses not to meditate, treating it as a burden, giving in to the monkey mind, or feeling you're doing it wrong. If you treat meditation like a burdensome chore you have to do, you most likely will feel resistance toward it and begin making excuses not to do it. However, if you can treat meditation as a method of rest and rejuvenation of your mind, body, and spirit, it won't feel like a burden and you will instead begin welcoming it.

The key to meditation is becoming aware of your focus and concentration. When we sit for meditation, and we fall into monkey mind, we begin thinking about everything our mind can conjure rather than focus. When this occurs, we acknowledge that this has happened, release the thought we were caught up in, and return our minds to the point of focus. Many people will begin judging themselves that they're doing it wrong or cannot meditate because of monkey mind. On the contrary! By acknowledging and being conscious of monkey mind and returning our focus, we are on the right track for meditation. We are training ourselves to focus, and we aren't going to be masters of meditation right away.

An Open-Minded Attitude

The most significant key that you will ever have to unlock meditation, psychic ability, magick, or energy work is your attitude. More specifically it is an attitude often referred to as a "beginner's mind." The truth is, there is no such thing as mastery of these fields, if by "mastery" we mean "learning everything there is and having nothing further to learn, gain, or experience." These areas are lifelong practices and studies. When someone falsely believes they know everything there is to know about these subjects, they've made an unconscious decision to stop their development and growth. The beginner's mind is an attitude of enthusiasm and openness, and an ability to learn more about something as if they are entirely new to these fields. This also prevents these practices from growing old, becoming boring, or having any development go dormant. Think again of children when they're learning something new that excites and fascinates them. This is beginner's mind.

German occultist Jan Fries states that "real magick is not merely an assortment of skills and techniques. It's more like an open-minded attitude, a blend of interest and dedication, which allows each honest mage to observe, to learn, to adapt, and to invent unique ways of changing identity and reality from within."[7]

With any spiritual or metaphysical practice, you reap what you sow. In other words, the more time, energy, and dedication that you invest in developing and maintaining these practices, the greater your results will be. In this way, think of it like working out. The more regularly you work out, the better your health and fitness will be. Eventually, you'll be able to advance to heavier weights, longer and faster runs, etc. However, if you begin to slack off for a period or become overconfident about what you can do when you approach these things again, you can burn yourself out or even hurt yourself. By keeping a beginner's mind and attitude, you can prevent yourself from falling out of a disciplined routine or burning out.

A common thing that happens with people when they begin meditation is that they'll start to fall asleep, no matter how hard they try to stay awake, and this has happened to me as well. About ten years ago, when I would take on these advanced courses on energy work and psychic ability, this would happen to me. You would have thought someone had drugged me. I was so enthusiastic and slightly arrogant about what I could do if I pushed myself. About five minutes into each session I would begin falling into a deep sleep and would wake up right as the exercise was ending. However, I would never fall asleep when the meditations were much more straightforward, even though the duration of the training was the same. One theory I heard that I resonate with is that this occurs when people are taking on more psychic activity or energy than they can handle and process. So to cope with it, the

---

7. Jan Fries, *Visual Magick: A Manual of Freestyle Shamanism* (Oxford, UK: Mandrake, 1992), 137.

mind tells itself to fall asleep and to disregard what it is doing in an act of self-preservation.

It's beneficial to be in an environment where you're entirely undisturbed and feel completely relaxed. If you choose to meditate inside, you will want to ensure that all your electronic devices and distractions such as phones are turned off or not in the environment at all. A cluttered or messy room will make it harder to feel relaxed and at peace. You also want a place with a bit of natural lighting and a fresh flow of air. Creating an atmosphere that feels psychologically peaceful is also beneficial. You may want to listen to soothing instrumental music, or light incense. Alternatively, you may find music and incense distracting. Everyone is a bit different in what calms them. If you choose to meditate outside, it's best to pick a place where you are all alone and where you won't be distracted by other people, devices, or sounds.

You will also want to ensure that you're physically comfortable. Make sure that you aren't wearing any clothing that feels restricting, binding, or uncomfortable. It's best to sit down with your feet on the ground or, if you prefer, you may want to sit on the ground with your legs crossed under you. Regardless of how you sit, you want to ensure that your spine is straight and that your head and shoulders aren't slumping.

Exercise 4

Learning to Focus with Basic Meditation

Begin by sitting in a comfortable position somewhere that you won't be disturbed. Make sure that your legs and arms aren't crossed unless you're intentionally sitting on the floor in a cross-legged position. Set a timer for five minutes. Close your eyes and breathe. Don't try to force your breath or to control it. Just breathe in a way that feels natural to you. Bring your awareness to your breathing. Follow it with your intention as the air flows in and out of your body. Notice how your body responds to breath. Trace its path inside of your body with every inhalation. Focus on nothing except your breath. If you start to think about other things, your mind begins to wander, and that monkey brain tries acting up, just return to your breathing without scolding or criticizing yourself.

Try meditating like this at least once a day. Slowly build up to ten minutes, then twenty, then half an hour. It may feel like a struggle at first, and there will be days when you really feel resistant to meditating at all, but it's important to keep with the practice of daily meditation to build your ability to focus. Your mind will wander many times. This isn't inherently a good or bad thing. It's part of the process of understanding how your mind works and how to override what it wants to do undisciplined. Whenever your mind wanders don't see it as failing, see it as succeeding in meditation. If this meditation were a workout, your wandering thoughts would be the weight you're lifting. You don't scold yourself for the weight being heavy. You lift it. You don't berate yourself for having wandering thoughts, you acknowledge them and bring your focus back to your breath, breathing naturally.

Exercise 5

Treasure Chest for Stress

The treasure chest for stress is a technique I developed based on a method I learned for Tibetan Dream Yoga. This technique relaxes you and can be used not only to help with psychic ability before a session, but can also be used before bed as you fall asleep to help promote lucid dreaming and astral projection. The best part of this technique is that it's made to assist with problem-solving on a deep subconscious level to help remove more stress from your life.

Begin by sitting down, getting comfortable and closing your eyes. Perform the Preliminary Focus (exercise 1). Take a deep breath. As you exhale, feel your breath drawing out any stress or tension that you may be holding on to at the moment. Pretend that time is beginning to slow down. As time slows down, you become more aware of your inner being. As you become more aware of your spiritual nature, your surroundings begin to drift away and out of focus.

Imagine that there's a golden treasure chest in front of you that unlocks and opens. Out of the chest emerges a small whirlwind. Take a moment and quickly go through your day, as if it were on fast-forward from when you woke up until right now. As you go through the day, if there's anything that has stressed you out or that has upset you, focus on it. Take a deep breath and as you exhale imagine that situation leaving your body through your breath like a cloud.

Feel this cloud carrying all of your stress, anxiety, thoughts, and emotions about the situation as it floats over the chest. Visualize those feelings and thoughts as they're sucked into the whirlwind and into the treasure chest. Consciously acknowledge that you are letting it go for now. Repeat this technique until you've released all the stress from the day.

When you are finished, you may choose to open the chest. All the stress that you had put into the chest has been transformed into solutions. These solutions beam out of the treasure chest like a rainbow arching up in the air and falling all around you. Take a moment to feel a calmness and an inner strength to take on the challenges of life. Know that the treasure chest has infused the circumstances with solutions that will allow you to solve them soon from a relaxed state. See the treasure chest close and lock.

Focused Flow, Not Force

Learning to relax deeply enhances our quality of life in such a stressful world. Learning to relax is the first step when you want to begin engaging in meditation or energy work. After calming the body one then eases the mind to start tapping into a focused state of consciousness, eliminating any mental background noise. Clarity of the body is crucial for clarity of the mind, emotions, and will.

Relaxation is an integral part of any psychic work. Relaxation puts us in a state of non-attachment where we aren't holding on to things that will hinder our telepathic reception. By relaxing our body and mind, we are releasing emotional, mental, and physical distractions. Being in a state of relaxation allows for receptivity and clarity, which opens us to a state of mindfulness. Mindfulness promotes awareness, and awareness is the key to wisdom.

One of the biggest pitfalls I find when someone begins pursuing psychic development is that they try entirely too hard. I don't mean that they're putting too much effort into the development itself. What I mean is they tend to try to force the unfolding of psychic ability by pushing themselves too hard with the exercises, techniques, and meditations. Psychic ability relies on a mentally relaxed state of detachment. A flower doesn't bloom through being pried open by force; likewise, psychic receptivity cannot be achieved through strain. Psychic receptivity comes with a state of mental passivity while simultaneously staying focused and open. We open ourselves up through relaxation. We want a focused flow, not force.

By relaxing, we remove our own internal distraction and become much better at discerning what we are receiving and what is coming from ourselves. By regularly relaxing and meditating we begin to fall into a regular state of relaxation and mindfulness even under the most chaotic circumstances. But while learning to relax and meditate we want to ensure that our environment is also supportive of this state of mind. Here are two different relaxation exercises to experiment with. You may find one works better for you than another.

Exercise 6

∽

Cocoon of Relaxation

Take a moment to stretch and then find a comfortable position—you may lie down if you feel drawn to. Focus on your breath. Breathe deeply, slowly, and rhythmically. Don't struggle. Find a pace that is comfortable for you.

With each inhalation, visualize yourself drawing in a calming energy of peace. With each exhalation imagine yourself blowing any stress or tension out of your body. The stress begins to fly away like dandelion seeds in the wind, floating away and bringing you more and more clarity.

Visualize an orb of light at your feet. The sphere is a very calm white and light mint color. It has a quality to it which is airy, icy, hot, and tingly. It is deeply soothing and healing. Anywhere it touches completely relaxes with your will.

Begin moving the orb upward to your shoulders, relaxing every muscle that it touches—front and back. When it gets to your shoulders, move the globe down each arm and hand—relaxing every muscle that it reaches. Draw the orb up your neck to your face—resting your eyes, your jaw, your facial muscles.

Listen to your body—where is there any discomfort, tension, or pain? Bring the orb to this area and as you draw in your breath, visualize your breath filling this area. Affirm that your body relaxes with your intentions.

Bring the orb back to your feet where it becomes a blanket of energy. Begin pulling this blanket up and around your body in your Witch Eye— like a cocoon of relaxation. When you are completely covered in your relaxation cocoon, visualize it beginning to melt and soak into your skin, deep throughout your muscles, into your nerves, and into your bones—giving you an even broader sense of relaxation.

Exercise 7

∞

Star Relaxation

Begin by sitting down, getting comfortable, and closing your eyes. Take a deep breath. As you exhale, feel your breath drawing out any stress or tension that you may be holding on to at the moment. Pretend that time is beginning to slow down. As time slows down, you become more aware of your inner being. As you become more aware of your spiritual nature, your surroundings begin to drift away and out of focus. Perform the Treasure Chest for Stress Technique (exercise 5).

Once you are feeling mentally and emotionally relaxed, begin to visualize a white star above your head glowing and pulsating with luminescent prismatic rays of the rainbow. From the star, a liquid light begins to pour down that looks like a beautiful opal, white and refracting different prismatic hues.

The liquid light falls upon the crown of your head, and as if it were a calming warm honey or warm wax relaxing everything it touches, it begins to cover your head, face, and neck, completely easing any tension in these areas. The liquid light begins to pour down your shoulders, chest, and upper back, relaxing and releasing any discomfort or tension. It continues to pour down to your stomach and lower back, your arms and hands. It's relaxing and releasing any stress you may feel.

Finally, the liquid light covers your lap, your legs, and your feet, bringing them into complete comfort. You're now completely covered in this liquid light. As if it were Tiger Balm, it begins to lightly tingle and soothes any aches or pains you may be feeling.

As if rewinding the process, the liquid light begins reversing direction, moving back up your feet, legs, lap, hands, arms, lower back and stomach, upper back and chest, shoulders, neck, face, and head. It then flows back up into the star and entirely off of your body. Now take a deep breath and mentally scan your body, releasing any tension you might still be feeling within it.

Exercise 8

❧

The Psychic Dimmer

One of the most challenging obstacles for the sensitive person is learning how to control the constant input of information and even mute it at times. Taking on the energy of others is draining and leaves us susceptible and vulnerable. Part of mastering the self and psychic senses is learning how to create boundaries and figuring out what is yours and what is from others. The following is a super handy technique used to take control of the situation energetically. This can also be used if the psychic information you're receiving is too quiet and you want to increase it, or if you're doing meditation, psychic work, or energy work and the external energy is too invasive or "loud" and you're having trouble relaxing and concentrating. This is a technique that I learned from Irma Kaye Sawyer that I've adapted.[8]

Begin by taking a few deep relaxing breaths. Envision a light dimmer switch before you. This light dimmer switch increases or decreases psychic sight and volume. Just like a dimmer switch or a volume knob, if you turn the knob to the right, the information increases, and if you set the knob to the left, the information decreases. Affirm this mentally to yourself. Take a moment and discern whether you feel you perceive energy too much or too little. With intent, turn the knob in the appropriate direction, willing the energy bombardment to increase or decrease.

Another variation of this technique is to see a faucet above you filling your aura with psychic information. Just like the dimmer, see a faucet handle before you. Affirm to yourself that this faucet can increase or decrease the flow of psychic information filling your auric field. Take a moment to discern whether you feel you perceive too much or too little psychic information. With intent, turn the faucet handle in the appropriate direction, willing the energy bombardment to increase or decrease.

---

8. Irma Kaye Sawyer, *The Brightstar Empowerments: Compilation Edition* (self-published, 2016), 28–29.

The Breath of Life

Breath is the bridge between the energies of the external world and the energies of your internal world. Breathing unites the internal and the external, creating a connection and circuit of energy flow. The word "spirit" comes from the Latin word for breath, which is *spiritus,* and was often used figuratively to refer to the spirit. The idea that breath itself is life force has parallels in various cultures, where it is known as prana, ruach, mana, telesma, chi, ki, numen, orgone, pneuma, od, and odic force.[9] By working with our breath, we are working directly with life-force energy. Certain types of breathwork can cool down and relax the body and mind, while others can warm up and excite the body and mind, by changing the speed of the body's rhythms.

Conscious breathing can help cultivate a deep-rooted connection with and enjoyment of life. By working with our breath, we can achieve more advanced states of meditation and consciousness. Since breathing is something so subtle and usually automatic, by tuning in to it we can strengthen our mind's ability for concentrating and perceiving things that are of a subtler nature.

Exercise 9

Elemental Square Breathing

Square breathing (sometimes called the four-fold breath in yoga practices) is an effortless technique. This type of breathing cultivates a sense of balance, centeredness, and stillness. For this reason, I also tap into the four elemental forces while performing this breathing technique. That way I'm placing myself even deeper into an inner and outer connective balance with the elemental powers that permeate all things.

Perform the Star Relaxation exercise. Inhale through your nose a long and steady breath to the count of four while mentally thinking the name of each element during each beat of a count:

"Earth, Air, Fire, Water."

---

9. Christopher Penczak, *The Inner Temple of Witchcraft: Magick, Meditation and Psychic Development* (Woodbury, MN: Llewellyn Publications, 2013), 78–81.

Hold the breath inside of your filled lungs for the count of four while mentally thinking the name of each element during each beat of a count:

"Earth, Air, Fire, Water."

Exhale through your mouth a long and steady breath to the count of four while mentally thinking the name of each element during each beat of a count:

"Earth, Air, Fire, Water."

Hold the breath outside of your empty lungs for the count of four while mentally thinking the name of each element during each beat of a count:

"Earth, Air, Fire, Water."

Keep repeating until you feel a sense of calm, balance, and clarity.

Exercise 10

Solar Breathing

Solar Breathing is a variation of a breathing technique often referred to as "bellows breath" in yoga practices. Solar Breathing energizes and revitalizes your mind and promotes energy. This is a great technique to use if you're trying to raise your vibration or increase your energy levels, or if you are feeling a bit mentally hazy or fatigued. If at any time you begin to feel dizzy or light-headed, stop the technique, take a break, and then retry it with a bit of a slower and less intense inhalation and exhalation.

Perform the Star Relaxation exercise. You want to inhale deeply and a bit forcefully through your nose, making sure that you're expanding your stomach while inhaling to the count of one. As you inhale, you want to visualize the sun rising on the horizon quickly with the breath. Exhale deeply and a bit forcefully through your mouth, making sure that you're pulling your stomach inward while exhaling to the count of one. As you exhale, you want to visualize that the sun is setting on the horizon quickly with the breath. Repeat this ten times. Take a break and rest for a moment until your breath returns to its average pace. This usually takes about thirty seconds. Do another set of ten breaths and then another rest. Repeat one more set of ten breaths to finish.

Exercise 11

Lunar Breathing

Lunar Breathing is a variation of the Elemental Square Breathing technique. Lunar Breathing helps to calm your body and mind deeply and slow down your mind. This is a great technique to use if you're trying to lower your vibration, decrease your energy levels, and are looking to perform a method of psychic ability such as clairvoyance or mediumship. Instead of breathing on the count of four to the names of the elements, you'll be visualizing the cycles of the moon to the count of six.

Perform the Star Relaxation exercise. Inhale through your nose a long and steady breath to the count of six. As you inhale, you want to visualize the moon in a state of waxing. That is you want to see it phase from a dark moon to a full moon. Hold the breath inside of your filled lungs for the count of six while visualizing a full moon. Exhale through your mouth a long and steady breath to the count of six while visualizing the moon in a state of waning. That is to say that you want to see it phase from full moon to dark moon. Hold the breath outside of your empty lungs for the count of six while visualizing the dark moon. Repeat six times.

Chapter 3
TUNING IN

O pening up to perceive and interact with subtle energies can drastically change your life; it can help you find clarity, bring peace into your life, empower yourself and others, and create effective change within our world. However, we shouldn't downplay either the responsibility that comes with this or the possible risks that come along with doing it improperly. I'm here to help guide you through safely opening yourself up to perceiving these energies as well as securely closing yourself off so that you're not being constantly bombarded with psychic information.

After learning how to relax the body and the mind through visualization and breathing, we can now focus on becoming receptive. To do so, we need to ensure that we're bringing all of our awareness inward and that we're operating in the alpha brainwave state. By tapping in to our inner worlds, we can affect our outer world. I call the following exercises, exercises 12 through 18, as a set "Tuning In." Two different images come to mind with the term "Tuning In." Just as you would tune a radio to the right station to receive the proper broadcast, we want to ensure that we're attuned to receive energetic information accurately. The other idea that comes to mind is the idea of tuning a guitar to make sure that it's playing the proper notes clearly; we want to ensure that we are transmitting and sending out our energetic information clearly.

These "Tuning In" exercises consists of grounding, raising terrestrial energy, drawing celestial energy, creating a circuit, centering, entering alpha, and setting a psychic prompt, done in that order. Likewise, "Closing Down" refers to exiting alpha, performing a psychic flush, calling back your energy, grounding, and centering, done in that order. Tuning in sets the stage to begin tapping in to the potential of your mind. With time and effort tuning in won't take as long as it does when establishing the practice. Every exercise in the book after this chapter will assume that you perform the Tuning In exercises at the beginning unless otherwise stated. Here we are establishing the practice to create a solid foundation on which all work in this book will be built.

Avoiding Burnout and Magickal Impact

For the past several years now I've spent the month of October giving psychic readings out of a witchcraft shop called Enchanted in Salem, Massachusetts. While this quaint little shop on Pickering Wharf is tucked away from the heart of the crowds of Essex Street during October, I cannot underplay the crowds or level of busyness. Salem, a town synonymous with witchcraft, both historically and for modern practices, attracts an estimated 250,000 visitors each year in what feels like a hybrid of Halloween and Mardi Gras.

As such, I'm reading people nonstop daily during this month, and seriously, it's nonstop. When I first began working there, I would be so opened up to psychic information from being in that state of consciousness all day that I found afterward that I would start reading everyone around me who wasn't coming in for a reading. Reading in this manner already puts you at the risk of burning out, but when you can't shut it down the feeling of burnout dramatically intensifies.

The grounding technique is named after electrical grounding. Essentially, electrical grounding is when you have an unused neutral wire that is used to take a current of electricity and direct it into the ground, so that excess and unneeded electricity has a safe outlet. This ensures that you don't cause a fuse to blow or trip a circuit breaker with all of the extra voltage. If someone were to touch an appliance or device that wasn't grounded, their body would take the impact of that electricity as if it were the grounding cord and leave them shocked. Just like with electrical power, if you don't ground yourself, you run the risk of working with more psychic or magickal energy than your system can handle, and you can damage yourself. Another way to think of grounding is to think of it as your release valve that relieves any excess energy. In many ways grounding is one of the most crucial forms of protection when it comes to working with energy.

I've also had what some refer to as "magickal impact" from not grounding and centering myself properly before taking on a magickal working that involves working with intense energies. Magickal impact is what it sounds like; it's coming into energies in a forceful collision. The symptoms of this are feeling like you've been whiplashed in a car crash, having flu-like body aches, a fogginess of mind, and a feeling of being drained immediately. Not only does it feel like the impact of a collision, but the experience has an impact upon the person.

Have you ever met an energy healer, psychic, or witch who seemed to be entirely out of their mind and out of touch with this world? This can be caused by not being well grounded, whereby they've fried themselves. Notice how some of them seem to be like those who've taken a bit too many psychedelics back in their day? The same term is used: "they've fried themselves." This is prolonged magickal impact without being remedied. Grounding also ensures that we don't burn ourselves out energetically. Too much energy can be damaging to the system. This can manifest in many ways, ranging from being spacey, dizzy, or aching, to, in some worse cases, physical illnesses and mental and emotional imbalances.

The body has natural ways of grounding itself but it is designed to only ground so much energy naturally without conscious intention. Digestion is one of the ways the body naturally grounds itself. Certain foods such as vegetables and fruits are beneficial for assisting your energetic perception and abilities, but for grounding, the best foods tend to be dark chocolate, carbohydrates, and red meats. However, we all have different dietary and health needs, so use your own discernment when it comes to food. For emergency grounding, it's recommended to place your feet, knees, hands, arms, and crown of your head on the floor or ground for a few minutes and imagine that all the excess energy in your system is flowing out into the ground safely. Sitting or lying down will also help ground you. Some also like to walk barefoot on earth or grass to ground themselves.

While grounding and centering are crucial for any healthy energy work, it's also beneficial in more mundane areas of life in which there's an energetic overload. This includes situations, people, or places that overwhelm or drain your energy. Situations where this may be helpful include large noisy groups; crowds of people; invasive emotional energies; intrusive sound (particularly loud music you dislike); when someone close to you is overly upset, sensitive or angry, and you're absorbing that energy; or when you're feeling extra spacey and generally ungrounded. For psychic and magick work, grounding techniques are sufficient to keep you safe and healthy in most circumstances.

Exercise 12

∽

Grounding

Make sure that your legs are planted firmly on the ground about shoulder width apart. Alternatively, if you're sitting on the ground, ensure that your legs are crossed. Take a moment to focus on your body, and feel all of the natural energy running throughout it. Bring your awareness to the top of your head, and slowly scan your body downward with your attention. As you reach your pelvis, imagine that your energy is running like roots through your legs. Keep scanning your body awareness, bring that sense of examining yourself down farther past your legs as you feel your energetic roots begin to gently dig into the ground. With a firm but relaxed sense of willpower, extend your energy down these roots below you. These roots are an extension of your energy body.

These roots begin traveling downward through the soil and bedrock, through the underground caves and pockets of air, through underground streams of water, and finally to the molten core. The molten core doesn't burn or cause any pain; instead, it soothes you even deeper as you feel its warmth with your energy. Your roots keep traveling through the molten core until they reach the very center, the heart of the earth. This heart is made of a beautiful bright white light. It is the source of infinite power, the soul and consciousness of the earth itself. This is one of the most important energies that you will ever come across as a witch. As you feel the white light inside of the earth's heart, you find that its energy is like a dream and a song. You take a moment to meditate on what that means, and to feel it deeply. The dream song of the earth is powerful, but a steady, secure, and anchored power—one that is self-regulating, ensuring that you are energized as much as you can handle. Any energy that you cannot handle is released through your roots, blessing and healing the earth and all its inhabitants. Take a moment to feel how fastened and secured you feel to the earth. You are grounded.

Figure 1: Grounding and Drawing Energy

Deeply Rooted and Branching Out

Grounding is an example of a practice that seems rudimentary on the surface, but is an exercise that is crucial to master and an exercise you should try to be mindful of throughout your day. You don't need to be doing any sort of energy work to ground yourself. Make an audit throughout your day any time you feel overwhelmed. Ask yourself how grounded you feel. Grounding ensures that we're not only secure in the amount of energy we're taking on (whether that's emotional, psychic, mental, physical, or any other type of energy); it also ensures that we're coming from a place of strength. Have you ever tried pulling weeds? The weeds with the strongest roots are the hardest to pluck from the earth. Trees have even stronger roots and since we're working with tree imagery here, I feel it's a powerful comparison. Ensuring that you're well grounded will also help you to become a stronger psychic witch. Practice the grounding technique several times. Get a really good feel for how you feel when you're grounded and how you feel when you're ungrounded.

Just like a tree, the deeper and stronger your roots, the more nutrients and water you can absorb. Having a strong grounding practice is more than just releasing energy; it's also a way to take in energy. This ensures that you aren't working with your own energy and depleting your natural energetic resources. Instead, with the next exercise, you'll be taking in external energy in a healthy manner from the earth to work with—just like a tree, part of whose energy source comes from above in the form of the sun, our local star. In the following two exercises we will be raising energy from the earth and drawing down energy from the stars. The earth and the heavens were revered as important complementary forces and as such are usually partnered together as deity consorts in ancient cultures. For example, the Greeks had Gaia and Uranus, and the Egyptians had Geb and Nut. In the *Rigveda* we find Dyaus Pita (the Sky Father) and Prithvi Mata (the Earth Mother). This motif is almost universal through civilization and is one of the most primal and archetypal forms of polarity across the board of drastically different but complementary forces.

As such, we're going to work with these two energies. After grounding you can perform the Raising Terrestrial Energy exercise and experience how it feels. You can then go from the Raising Terrestrial Energy exercise to the Drawing Down Celestial Energy exercise, or you can ground and skip Raising Terrestrial Energy and perform Drawing Down Celestial Energy instead. I recommend getting acquainted with how each one feels on its own before seeing how they feel together. After that we're going to create a circuit of these two energies so that they continually run through you. This way, you're empowered with external energy at your disposal without having to deplete your own.

Exercise 13

❧

Raising Terrestrial Energy

After you have a firm grasp of grounding, you will want to perform it again. This time we're going to raise the energy of the earth upward into our bodies. Bring your awareness back to the roots, down past the soil and bedrock, through the underground caves and pockets of air, through underground streams of water, past the molten core and deep into the glowing white light of the earth's heart. Begin soaking up this white light through your energetic roots, just as tree roots soak up water. Draw up the light through the lava and the underground streams and rivers of water, up through the caverns and air pockets, up through the bedrock and the fertile soil. Allow the earth's dream song to travel up through your whole body, energizing every cell.

Exercise 14

❧

Drawing Down Celestial Energy

Bring your awareness up through your body and feel your energy begin to extend beyond your shoulders and the crown of your head in a similar fashion to the way you did with your roots, but instead envision these as branches of a tree. Feel your awareness move up beyond your body and will these branches outward. They grow higher and higher sprouting leaves as they move upward, reaching the sky. The branches begin to overshadow you as they reach past the atmosphere and into space. The stars in the heavens start to twinkle and pulsate in acknowledgment of your presence reaching out to them.

This is pure celestial energy, the *Musica Universalis*, or music of the spheres, the song of harmonic resonance. You take a moment to meditate on what that means, and to feel it deeply. Celestial energy is one of the most essential energies that you will ever come across for psychic ability, as the astral energies of the stars see all and know all. They begin to glow brighter and brighter for you, filling the void of space with brilliant white light. Begin to soak in this energy through your leaves and branches as if photosynthesizing the energy. Draw the energy down through your leaves and branches back into your body, filling you with this celestial energy.

Exercise 15

❧

Creating a Circuit

Take a deep breath and expand your energetic awareness outward in both directions this time, upward and downward, reaching the different songs. Soak in their energy simultaneously and draw them back into your body. This time concurrently run the earth energy up through your branches to offer to the celestial energy while running the celestial energy down into the earth energy. Keep repeating this process, moving it up and down, passing through you as a conduit creating a circuit of power. You're a child of the earth and the starry heavens; you are a psychic witch. Bring your awareness back to your body, knowing that this circuit of energy is still in place and performing its job, even when your awareness is off of it.

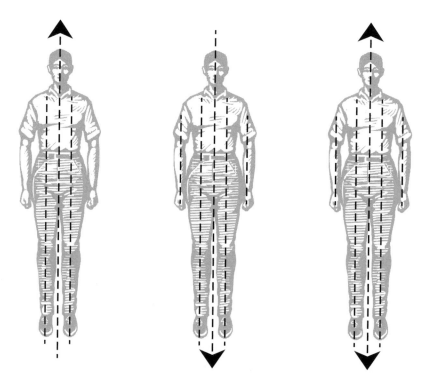

Figure 2: Creating an Energy Circuit

Energetic Stability

Centering is a meditation technique that is used to stabilize our internal energies, align us with higher universal energies, and create a relationship model of where we are in regard to everything else in existence, which creates a sense of presence. Just as we have a physical center of gravity within our body where all our mass seems to concentrate, we also have a spiritual center where all our energy focuses. This center is the heart center, which acts as a bridge between the higher and lower frequencies and our Higher Self and Lower Self. Centering is an act of focusing all of your attention, energy, and power on one central spot: the heart center. In the previous exercises, we have terrestrial energy running through our bodies from below and celestial energy running through our bodies from above, forming a circuit. Centering stabilizes these energies into a focused power source so that we can dynamically conjure energy.

Mystics and visionaries of different religions and spiritual paths have often proclaimed that "God is love" or that everything is composed of a Divine Love. Centering in the heart is communion with the Universe as the Divine Heart and Divine Mind. Witches refer to this state of connected centeredness as "perfect love and perfect trust." Centering is a paradoxical state of personal empowerment and surrender to the All. Perfect love is recognizing the divinity within all things in existence and understanding that there's a unifying force of intelligence that runs through and embodies everything, a numinous quintessence. Perfect trust is surrendering your personal egoic sense of self to the unified Universal Consciousness.

Many teachers of psychic ability and mediumship will focus on coming from a space of love to open up and receive information and to trust whatever they receive while in this heart-centered state. Perfect love and perfect trust is a similar idea, except we're working with putting ourselves in harmony with the love of the All and trusting the energy that we receive. We're tuning into a frequency that is beyond ourselves and our perception of what defines self, and bringing that awareness to a concentrated center within our hearts. We are taking the realms of inner and outer, above and below, other and self, and centering that as one space within ourselves. This embodies the Hermetic axiom of "As above, so below. As within, so without" and unifying it.

Centering also orients us by creating a sense of where we are in proximity to everything that exists in all of the cosmos. This sense of centeredness creates an attitude of what mystics refer to as "being here now." You can think of it in comparison to heliocentrism, the fact that all the planets revolve around our sun in the solar system, which is the central point around which they all orbit. Instead of the sun, it is our sense of self, and instead of the planets, it's the entire cosmos. Centering orients our perception as being the center of the Universe.

Exercise 16

Centering

Envision that you are the center of the cosmos. Everything in the Universe is in direct relationship to you as the central point. Bring your attention to the direction beneath your feet, reaching down to the very edge of the cosmos itself in that direction. Visualize a giant quartz crystal at the edge of the cosmos in the direction below you, glowing with prismatic iridescent brilliance. The crystal is pulsating with the Divine Love of quintessence. Envision that a steady beam of prismatic light quickly shoots from it and reaches up until it meets your feet, where it is then pulled up into your body until it reaches your heart center. Feel this Universal Love pulsate within your heart center, connecting you with the love that composes all reality.

Repeat this process of bringing your attention to a crystal at the edge of the Universe full of Universal Love for the following directions: before you, behind you, to your right, to your left, and above you.

Take a moment and feel the six rays of energy concentrated on your heart center all at once, infusing it with a sense of clarity, peace, balance, stillness, but most of all a sense of Universal Love. Any energy that feels like it's too much is drawn down effortlessly into your grounding cord. Know that your heart is the nexus of the cosmos itself, infused with a brilliant luminosity. Know that as the vision of the rays fades, you are still centered and all you have to do is focus on your heart as the center of reality to center yourself.

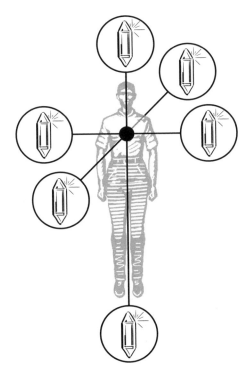

Figure 3: Centering Your Energy

Exercise 17

❧

Entering Alpha

There are various methods of entering the alpha brainwave state, but they all follow a relatively similar pattern of focusing on a mix of colors and imagery, making them vivid in your Witch Eye, and counting down slowly. Here is my favorite alpha technique that I've developed based on my studies with witchcraft elder Laurie Cabot in the Cabot Tradition of Witchcraft, and Christopher Penczak in the Temple of Witchcraft Tradition. They both have different methods of achieving the alpha brainwave state and this is my own, inspired by experimenting with their techniques.

Envision that you're in the middle of a clearing in the forest at night. You know that here you're completely protected and at peace within this forest, and you gaze up to see the full moon hanging above your head surrounded by stars adorning the night sky. The moon sends down a small faceted and polished jewel about three inches by three inches that descends and hovers before you. You begin to hear an ethereal and beautiful symphony of music overhead.

You lift your gaze to notice the aurora borealis above you in a beautiful crimson color. You watch as the northern lights dance and pulse in the night sky. The jewel before you begins reflecting this color, turning a vibrant ruby red color.

The aurora borealis shifts to a deep orange color. As you watch the northern lights dance and pulse in the night sky, you notice that the jewel before you begins reflecting this color, turning a warm amber orange color.

The northern lights shift color again, this time turning into a brilliant yellow color. As you watch the northern lights dance and pulse in the night sky, you notice that the jewel before you begins reflecting this color, turning a bright citrine yellow color.

Once again, the northern lights shift color, this time turning into a vibrant green color. As you watch the northern lights dance and pulse in the night sky, you notice that the jewel before you begins reflecting this color, turning to a vibrant emerald green color.

The northern lights shift color yet again, this time turning into a deep blue color. As you watch the northern lights dance and pulse in the night sky, you notice that the jewel before you begins reflecting this color, turning a deep sapphire blue color.

The northern lights shift color again, this time turning into a royal violet color. As you watch the northern lights dance and pulse in the night sky, you notice that the jewel before you begins reflecting this color, turning a royal amethyst color.

Once more, the northern lights shift color again, this time turning into a brilliant white color. As you watch the northern lights dance and pulse in the night sky, you notice that the jewel before you begins reflecting this color, turning a brilliant moonstone white color, with a radiance of the rainbow to it.

The aurora borealis fades away in the sky. You lower your gaze to the jewel before you. As you focus on the jewel it begins to pulse through all the colors: red, orange, yellow, green, blue, violet, and white. You start to count down, feeling yourself going deeper and deeper within yourself with each number: seven, six, five, four, three, two, one, zero. You are now in an alpha state of consciousness.

Exercise 18

Setting a Psychic Prompt

You may find that you don't have the time to fully enter into alpha to perform a psychic working or an act of instant magick while out and about, but still need to achieve the state. You can learn to condition yourself to enter alpha at any time. However, this should not be a substitution for entering alpha, but rather something you use day-to-day when you're out and about and can't close your eyes to enter alpha. It will only work if you regularly enter alpha and keep conditioning yourself properly to set the psychic prompt. This ties back into the idea of neuroplasticity, which I discussed in the section about affirmations. You're conditioning your brain to perform a certain way based on a strongly linked command. Physiologist Ivan Pavlov conducted experiments on conditioning. In his most famous test, he rang a bell every time he fed dogs. The dogs started associating the sound with food and eventually began salivating whenever they heard the bell, even in the absence of food. Psychic prompting is a way of telling your brain that you're entering the alpha brainwave state.

Begin by sitting down, getting comfortable, and closing your eyes. Tune in by repeating the exercises in this chapter from Grounding to Entering Alpha. Create a simple physical gesture that you want to use as your psychic prompt. Common ones include crossing your fingers or having one finger touch another. As witches we want our prompt to be something that seems ordinary and casual so we can perform magick or tap in to our psychic ability unnoticed by others. I strongly suggest crossing your fingers, as it's not only a subtle, undetectable movement but most people already associate it with the idea of a wish or hope for something to occur ("Fingers crossed!") or with being mischievous such as fingers crossed behind your back.

Hold this gesture (such as crossing your fingers) and affirm while in alpha:

"Whenever my two fingers are entwined
I will enter this current state of mind
Where the psychic flows and my magick grows."

Perform this exercise every time you enter alpha to keep strengthening the prompt's association. Whenever you need to enter alpha quickly, try using your prompt and see how your state of consciousness shifts. The more you perform this, the quicker you'll be able to enter alpha on command.

Brainwave Entrainment

Brainwave entrainment, also called brainwave synchronization, is a hypothesized theory that our brains have the ability to naturally synchronize to specific brainwave states through external stimuli in the form of pulsing lights, sound, or electromagnetic waves. The most common and accessible method of brainwave entrainment is in the form of binaural beats. While this is still a fringe theory and area of study, many psychics I know—myself included—believe in its ability to alter consciousness.

Binaural beats are when two different sound frequencies combine to give the illusion of a third one. To create a binaural beat, a consistent and unwavering tone is played in the left ear (let's say it's 200 Hz for example), while another steady tone is played in the right ear (let's say at 205 Hz). The brain will hear this as wavering sound and will process it as an entirely new frequency (which would be 5 Hz in our example) as if the two frequencies have given birth to a new one.

Binaural beats require a pair of good headphones and should never be used when you need to be in a state of alert awareness such as when you are driving. I suggest experimenting with different physical prompts for different brainwave states. For example, crossing your fingers for alpha and touching your thumb and index finger for theta. I don't suggest binaural beats as a replacement for entering alpha through meditation, as provided in the last section, but rather as a complementary method to further solidify the connection between brainwave states and your psychic prompts.

Closing Down

One of the most commonly asked questions that I receive is how to switch your psychic ability off. I can understand why this is commonly asked. In all the books I've read on psychic ability, and in all the courses I've taken on the subject, most talk about how to open up to psychic perception while almost none discuss how to close back down. Failing to teach how to close down your perception is something that I see as irresponsible. Let me be super clear: you should always close down any time you tune in, as soon as you are done performing your work. So if you're doing just one exercise, close down afterward. If you're doing several exercises together, close down after all your work has been performed. So while the exercises don't say to close down after this section, just assume that you are meant to. Failure to do so can lead to burnout, ungroundedness, exhaustion, mental fogginess, and overloaded senses. Always remember that you can use the Psychic Dimmer (exercise 8) to modify the level of input you're receiving at any time.

Exercise 19

Exiting Alpha

To exit alpha, simply close your eyes and focus on your body and environment while counting upward from zero to seven. Affirm that you're returning back to your regular state of consciousness. Slowly open your eyes and begin to move your body. Focusing on your body and your physical environment can help you to exit alpha.

It may also be helpful to create a physical prompt to help solidify when you're done with your psychic and magickal work. For example, I have a hematite ring that I wear on my left thumb. Whenever I perform a psychic reading I remove the ring to signal to myself subconsciously that I'm ready to enter a different state of consciousness. Likewise, when I'm done with the psychic reading or energy work I place the ring back on my thumb to re-emphasize that I'm done with that state of consciousness and ready to return to my regular state of consciousness. Finalize your exit of alpha by grounding yourself one last time.

Exercise 20

⤳

Psychic Cleanse

This is similar to the practices taught by Laurie Cabot ("Total Health Clearance") and Christopher Penczak ("Clearance and Balance"). This technique is used to release any energy that you may have taken on in the magickal working or the psychic reading. It's not uncommon to have absorbed some of the client's energy when interacting with them psychically or magickally. This technique ensures that you are releasing anything that isn't yours. This ensures that you aren't taking on any health symptoms, emotional states, or thought forms of the other person or of the magickal working you just performed.

Rub your hands together and visualize energy beginning to emanate from them. Visualize this energy coming out like a waterfall and feel the energy flowing out of the palms of your hands. Hold your hands a few inches behind your neck. Move your hands from the base of your neck over your head and down the front of your body; visualize it pushing through your body and flushing out any energy that doesn't belong to you. State,

"I release and clear out any energy that isn't mine."

Exercise 21

⤳

Calling Back Your Energy

An additional technique I like to perform is to call back my energy. Just as you take on the energy of other people or environments, you can also lose some of your energy. By performing the psychic cleanse and then calling back your energy, you are ensuring that everyone's energy has been appropriately sorted and returned to its proper owner.

Bring your attention to a few feet above your head and visualize a silver ball about the size of your fist floating above it. Imagine that you're writing your name across the silver ball with a black marker. As you do so, the silver ball begins to glow with silver and begins to act like a magnet. It begins drawing to itself any energy that you have misplaced during the reading or energy work. It brings back your energy from the subject of your reading or the person you may have been healing. It brings back the energy that you may have lost to the environment around you. It begins bringing back fragments of yourself that you have lost throughout space and time or other dimensions of reality.

When you have completed this, take a deep breath and feel and visualize the silver ball beginning to glow gold. Imagine that it is starting to shine down upon you. It begins returning all of the energetic pieces of yourself to your body and your auric field as if it is raining down upon you and absorbing back into you. Mentally state to yourself, "I am whole." Take a moment to feel what wholeness feels like. Ground any excess energy that is neither yours nor your client's back down into the earth.

Exercise 22

Balancing and Re-Polarizing

This exercise is used to see how balanced and polarized you are energetically. It ensures that you're in complete balance mentally, emotionally, spiritually, and physically. I perform this after any psychic or magickal working, or when I'm feeling off and am not sure why.

Tune in. Take a deep breath and state:

"I summon the scales of mind."

Envision golden scales before you, like the scales that Lady Justice holds. Reach your hands out as if they are right in front of you, placing one hand under each scale. Feel how they feel. Is one heavier than the other? Is one side of the scale lower than the other? Now affirm:

"I balance and polarize all of my mental energy."

As you say this, move your hands as if you are leveling out the scales before you, knowing that you're bringing balance and polarity to your mind. Repeat this process, summoning the scales of the body, the scales of spirit, and the scales of emotion.

Chapter 4
EXTRASENSORY PERCEPTION

There are five main categories in which extrasensory perception is experienced: clairvoyance, clairtangency, clairaudience, clairgustance, and clairalience. Almost any psychic phenomenon can fit into these five main categories because they are extensions of the five ways in which we perceive reality in general: through seeing, feeling, hearing, smelling, and tasting. The clair perceptions can be both internal and external, which we will explore together.

We are all born with a predisposition toward one of the psychic senses. This makes that extrasensory perception the easiest to work with. On the other hand, we also have some psychic senses that are more underdeveloped than others—sometimes to the point of that ability being completely dormant, with those senses wholly blocked and hidden from us. These are the noirs I talked about earlier. Do not worry; it's not that you aren't "gifted" with them and will not ever have them. They're just dormant, waiting to be reawakened.

When you have a psychic sense that isn't naturally strong, you have to work and work at it. It may take a few days, a few months, or even a few years to reawaken depending on how seriously and consistently you practice on working at them. Think of it as working out these senses. Just as they say in the gym, "no pain, no gain" and "you lose what you don't use." Both are equally true when it comes to psychic ability; however, you never entirely lose any of the psychic senses, they simply go into a state of dormancy since your mind believes that you don't need them to function in mundane reality.

Exercise 23

Spell to Awaken Psychic Abilities

For this spell all you will need is a clear wine glass filled with some cold water. Perform it upon the full moon, and I recommend doing it once a month to keep charging and strengthening your abilities. You will need to perform this spell outside. If the full moon is not visible due to weather, do not worry; it will still work.

Perform the Tuning In exercises. Begin Lunar Breathing. Hold the glass up above your head so that the moonlight is shining through the glass. If it's cloudy outside, simply raise it in the general direction of where the moon most likely is. See how the moon's light fills the wine glass. While holding the glass up to the moon, recite:

"By lunar light I charge this water
Asking of blessings, that it may alter
All of my senses to enhance and extend
With a mind to interpret and comprehend"

Bring the glass down to your brow to your Witch Eye and recite:

"So that I may see more clearly
Touch and feel more sincerely
Taste and smell more distinctly
Hear and know more succinctly"

Bring the glass down to your chest at your heart area and recite:

"I drink of the moon and take in the power
As a psychic witch I declare in this hour
All my senses that are normally concealed
Are stirred and awakened and hereby revealed"

Drink all the water, allowing the blessings of the moon to soak and absorb into your body.

Exercise 24

The Black Roses

Perform the Tuning In exercises. Envision a beautiful garden full of beautiful birdsong. You see a rose bush in front of you. In your Witch Eye, rise and walk toward it. As you get closer you notice that all of the petals of each rose are a deep black. Take a moment to appreciate the unique beauty of these roses. Look at the thorny stems, the leaves, and the flowers. Feel the warm glow of the sun on your skin.

Run your hand along the roses, feeling their silky petals. Run your hands along the stems, touching the thorns. Pick one of the flowers from the stem and smell its beautiful floral fragrance. It smells like a rose, but much more luxurious than any other rose you've ever smelled, and also has its own distinct, unique smell. Now, bite into the flower. As you do, you realize to your surprise that it has a deeply rich, chocolaty taste. Take a moment to savor the flavor. As the chocolate taste begins to fade from your tongue, you're filled with a deep sense of wellness and happiness. You notice that where you bit into the flower is beginning to regrow back into perfect form as if you never bit into it.

Take the flower and place it back from where you plucked it. Miraculously, the flower becomes part of the rose bush again as if you never took it off to begin with. As it re-merges with the flower you hear a heavenly sound coming from everywhere and nowhere all at once, and a quiet voice coming from the rosebush thanks you.

Allow the vision to fade.

Now take a moment to rate each clair sense on a scale of one to ten, ten being perfect clarity and one being the inability to conjure the sense. This will help you to get an idea of where your natural strengths are and where you need to put extra work into it.

Clairvoyance: Seeing the garden, seeing the black roses, being able to pick the rose, watch it regenerate, and place it back upon the rose bush

Clairtangency: Feeling the sun on your skin, the silky rose petals, the stems and the thorns, the emotional feeling of wellness and happiness

Clairgustance: The taste of the flower in your mouth

Clairalience: The smell of the roses

Clairaudience: The sound of birdsong, the heavenly sound, the small voice thanking you

Clairvoyance

Clairvoyance is experienced in two different ways: internal clairvoyance and external clairvoyance. Internal clairvoyance is the ability to see something on the screen of your mind. Internal clairvoyance is experienced with symbolism and visions. External clairvoyance is the ability to see an overlay of vision over your regular sensory sight, such as auras, spirits, orbs, sparks, and shadows. I'm predisposed to being naturally external clairvoyant. People are usually pretty surprised when I tell them that internal clairvoyance is something I've had to work at to strengthen to the point of being consistently clear and vivid.

With internal clairvoyance, there are three main points of view to be aware of, particularly when it comes to visions, journey work, or meditation: first, second, and third person. First-person point of view sees the vision as if the situation is happening to you. Second-person point of view sees the vision as if it's happening to someone else and you're watching it as a bystander—present, but not the primary person the vision is centered around. Third-person point of view is when you are completely removed from the situation while you're viewing it. This is usually like watching a movie on the screen of your mind.

The Screen of Your Mind

The screen of your mind is the place where you visualize from your Witch Eye. Most people think that they "see" the images inside of their heads, but when they home in, they usually discover that it takes up spatial area outside of their head. This location is usually six inches to a foot in front of and slightly above their heads. Since you've been reading this, you're probably already in a light alpha brainwave state (reading does this) and the words you're reading are creating images in your head. So let's try something.

I want you to think of a pink unicorn running through a meadow, leaving behind it a streak of a rainbow. From reading that line of text, you most likely had an image quickly flash of the unicorn on the screen of your mind, even if it was just for a split second. Where was it? Try to locate internally and externally where the image flashed.

Let's try again. I want you to think of a black and red dragon clawing angrily out of a volcano. Where was that? Same place? Different? Try it by conjuring up the visualization of several different images. As I said before, reading can put you into a light alpha brainwave state, so those who read novels tend to be able to conjure up the images stronger than others. Audiobooks work just as well as novels. I'm not a big novel reader; I tend to prefer metaphysical and occult books, but will read a fantasy novel if I'm looking to strengthen my visualization skills. Those who work with the visual arts tend to be stronger at conjuring up inner visions as well.

Visualization is also a magickal tool. By visualizing certain things with clarity we direct energy. When we visualize ourselves shielded, it's not so much the actual visualization that is shielding us. Instead the visual image relays information to the subconscious and the three souls of what you intend to do. The subconscious understands that you're looking for magickal or psychic protection and thereby empowers that intention and thus performs the protection itself. I cannot stress enough how important visualization skills are to magick and to opening up clairvoyance.

Figure 4: The Screen of Your Mind

Exercise 25

Visualization

To strengthen your inner clairvoyance, you're going to want a simple object that you can hold in your hand. I like to use a crystal because they tend to be simple in form and of a single predominant color. I like to use that as a good starting point for visualization strengthening. Put yourself in a meditative state and take in all of the shape, facets, and color. Turn it around in your hand to see every perspective of the crystal. Soak in every detail of the crystal that you can. Close your eyes and try to remember what it looks like. Try to conjure the image in your mind, trying to retain its color and shape.

The key here is to not try too hard. If you try to force the visualization, it's going to be a lot harder. Instead, you want to be in a really relaxed meditative state and approach this with a very playful and receptive attitude. You want to be in that alpha brainwave state of consciousness that is very daydreamy and relaxed. When you try forcing it with your Witch Eye, it tends to do the opposite; it becomes much harder to visualize. When you're done, open your eyes and study the crystal again and keep repeating this process of studying and recreating the image in your Witch Eye. When you're done with this, you want to close your eyes and conjure the image of it again. This time while you see the picture of the crystal in your Witch Eye, begin to change the color and shape of the crystal. Try turning the crystal into something else entirely.

Another great exercise is to use a picture, particularly one that has some sort of landscape or location; it doesn't matter if the image is a realistic photo of a place or a surreal fantasy location. Study the picture and recreate that image in your Witch Eye with your physical eyes closed. This is going to take practice, so keep going back and forth as you did with the last exercise. Now, while holding the image clearly in your Witch Eye, imagine yourself inside of the picture. Imagine what the picture would look like as a three-dimensional world that you are within. Take in your surroundings.

Exercise 26

Psychic Activation by Candle Flame

In this exercise, you are retraining your eyes to see energy. For this, you will need a candle that will be placed directly in front of you. It doesn't matter if the candle is at eye level or lower. Any candle will do, but if you want to go the extra mile a blue or purple candle will add extra oomph to this working. Perform this exercise at nighttime in a dimly lit room.

Begin by performing the Tuning In exercise. Light the candle. As you do, declare out loud:

> *"On this night, by candlelight*
> *I activate my Witch's Sight."*

Begin to perform the Lunar Breathing exercise. This will put you into a fairly light trance state. With a soft, relaxed gaze, focus upon the candle flame. Don't look directly at the flame, instead just allow your eyes to zone out as if you are looking through and past the candlelight. You should begin to see a warm golden glow surrounding the candle. Remember to keep breathing deeply. As the glow appears, keep your soft gaze fixed upon the glow and not the flame of the candle.

Keep staring in this trance state for a few minutes. Now and then re-affirm:

> *"On this night, by candlelight,*
> *I activate my Witch's Sight."*

Then close your eyes. You should see the glow of the light imprinted before you. Visualize it stimulating your Witch Eye upon your brow and moving inward to your pineal gland. As you do this, state out loud:

> *"The All-Seeing Eye is within me,*
> *and through it, I can clearly see,*
> *All that is hidden, all that is concealed,*
> *And all that is beyond the Veil revealed.*
> *All that is cloaked in Land, Sea, and Sky*
> *By Second Sight unveiled by Witch Eye."*

Open your eyes and repeat this process three times. When you are done with this exercise, extinguish the candle.

Witch Eye Cleansing and Charging

Sometimes our Witch Eye needs a bit of cleansing and charging. Think of it in a similar manner as glasses. When we wear glasses there's a strong chance that they're going to get smudged or fogged up. If you're having difficulty seeing something clearly with your Witch Eye, it may indicate that it needs to be cleansed and charged. While the pineal gland and the Witch Eye are one and the same, we can distinguish between the two because the Witch Eye is more of a sensation on the brow, and the pineal gland is the "eye within the eye" of the Witch Eye, located inside the brain.

Tune in. You are also going to perform the Centering exercise. However, this time instead of centering the energy to your heart, center it all on your pineal gland, which is located directly in the middle of your brain, slightly higher than your physical eyes. Visualize the pineal gland as a pea-sized eyeball with a pearl-colored iris resting in your mind and looking straight outward in front of you. Keep centering all of your energy here. Now you're going to perform the Entering Alpha exercise with a few modifications. Instead of the jewel disappearing at the end, keep seeing it run through each color of the rainbow. The jewel begins to turn black as if black were a light. Take a moment to visualize what black light might look like.

With your eyes still closed, roll your eyes upward as if you were trying to see something in back of your head, and keep your eyes like this. Visualize the jewel sending out a clockwise spiral beam of black light. It begins tracing a spiral on your forehead, awakening and stirring your Witch Eye. See an eyelid appear here and as the light keeps tracing a spiral on your forehead the eyelid opens up, revealing your Witch Eye. The Witch Eye's iris is entirely white. The spiral moves into and beyond the Witch Eye, moving deep inside your head until it hits the pineal gland. Feel the synchronization occurring between your Witch Eye and your pineal gland. This is cleansing and clearing all blockages to your Witch Eye and pineal gland.

The spiral beam slows down and steadies into a laser-like ray of light coming from the jewel through your Witch Eye and into your pineal gland. The jewel turns red, and the beam being emitted turns red also. As this red light soaks into your Witch Eye and pineal gland, the irises of both turn red. The jewel goes through each of the colors, shifting the color of the light and in turn affecting the color of the iris: red, orange, yellow, green, blue, purple, white, and then black. The jewel stops emitting its light and dissolves before you. Your Witch Eye and pineal gland's irises begin shifting through all the colors again until the irises are rainbow-hued, taking in a much broader spectrum of sight. Your Witch Eye and the eye-within-the-eye are now cleansed, charged, and synched up.

Exercise 28

Seeing Basic Auric Energies

Simply put, an aura is a bubble of life-force energy that surrounds a person. The aura is actually composed of several different layers, and we'll learn more about each one later on in the book. With clairvoyance we can perceive the aura's different layers as well as colors and shapes and forms within it.

To see auras and spirits and raw energy, you'll want to put yourself in a very relaxed meditative state of consciousness. Performing Elemental Square Breathing may be of assistance here. You'll want to keep that very soft gaze that you used with the Candle Flame exercise. You want to make sure that your vision is completely relaxed and you're not focusing in on anything specific. Try to see with the whole spectrum of your eyesight, taking in all the sights in front of you and your peripheral vision (which is what is seen on the sides of you by the eye when still looking straight ahead).

Just begin soaking in all the visual information in a very passive and receptive state of mind. Place your hand in front of you. This will work better if the lighting is low and you have a solid color surface serving as a background for this exercise. You can use the floor or the wall as the background. Black or white surfaces serve best, but any will work as long as they're a single color. Once you build this ability, it won't matter what the background is.

With this gaze, hold your hand out and look at it. Try to look past your hand as if your hand were a window that you see through and beyond. Look beyond any object to see its aura. As you practice this the etheric body of the aura will begin to emerge. This usually appears as a translucent, white, or gray haze or light around the hand. Often, it will be close to the hand itself and outlining it. To see beyond the etheric layer of the aura, start zooming out even further with your focus and bring your attention to a more significant part of the area surrounding your hand without focusing on anything.

Exercise 29

Seeing the Aura's Colors and Spirits

Sometimes people have trouble seeing color within auras. One of the ways to work around this is to project your thoughts to create a conversation with the Universe. A lot of times we have a hard time seeing things we haven't seen or experienced before. The mind likes to have frames of reference for non-physical things and uses this for all its psychic perception, so if you've never seen a full colorful aura before, it's going to be harder to see it than if your mind has a frame of reference to compare and interpret the information.

Once you begin seeing the aura in the last exercise, internally ask "what color would this aura be?" without overthinking it. Most likely, you aren't going to see the color in front of you immediately. Trust whatever comes to you first. Trust the first thought or instinct. Now, while staring at the aura, start using your visualization techniques to fill in the color. For example, if I were staring at the aura and I asked, "What color is this?" and what came to me was blue, I would stare at the aura and begin projecting a visualization of blue as the aura.

By creating this process of projecting and receiving what the color may be, you start establishing communication between your subconscious mind, conscious mind, and the Universe about how to perceive these auras. Some who have internal clairvoyance mastered over external clairvoyance find that it's easier to close your eyes, recreate what you're seeing and envision the color of the aura around it. To begin synching your internal and external clairvoyance, keep switching between visualizing it internally and externally by opening your eyes and seeing the aura and closing your eyes to see the color. Slowly increase the speed between open and close sight until you're blinking your eyes rapidly. This should help bring that inner vision outward.

You may also be surprised to notice that the color you're projecting on the aura may change. So perhaps I was projecting blue on the aura, but instead, I start seeing violet. Don't force it to become blue; this is most likely your Higher Self making corrections to your perception. This also goes for energy. You may see sparks, shadows, or flashes of color with this type of vision and that's completely normal. Usually, that will help you to look past the veil and into the other realms and our neighbors who cohabitate this multidimensional reality with us. But it all starts with being able to see the etheric field of the aura and building on that.

Clairtangency

Clairtangency is clear feeling. Clairtangency can range from palpable psychic sensations within or on the body to psychometry; the ability to touch an object and gain information about it is a form of clairtangency. It is a tactile psychic perception. Feeling like someone has touched you, feeling an increase or decrease in temperature in your body, feeling pain or pleasure, feelings of disease, gut feelings, goosebumps, feeling spider-web sensations, and tingling are all forms of clairtangency. If there are any physical sensations perceived by the body in regard to psychic information, then it is clairtangency. Clairtangency tends to be one of the most natural forms of psychic ability. However, most people are out of touch with their bodies and more in touch with their mental processes. By learning to listen to your body and how it reacts to things, you will be able to get more in touch with your clairtangent abilities.

Clairtangency mainly operates from the hands. Awakening your hands to feel and direct energy is beneficial for both psychic and magickal practices. Traditionally witches divide their body into two sides, projective and receptive or sun-side and moon-side. The projective hand (or sun hand) is the hand in which you direct energy, just as the sun projects light. The receptive hand (or moon hand) is the hand in which you receive or feel the energy from, just as the moon receives and reflects the sun's light.

The easiest way to determine which hand is your projective hand is simply by figuring out if you're right-handed or left-handed. A great analogy to understand this is by imagining that you're a baseball player, who has one hand with a mitt in which they catch the ball, and another free hand with which they throw. If you're ambidextrous, you could simply just choose a hand to be your projective hand, but traditionally projective would be your right hand and receptive would be your left hand. This is why when calling in a directional element or a deity, witches will raise their left hand, to invite the energy into their space, and raise their right hand when releasing and sending off energy. The left hand brings energy in, the right hand pushes it out.

Exercise 30

Awakening the Hands

Tune in. Perform the Solar Breathing exercise. As you inhale, envision energy spiraling up around you, and on the rapid exhalations, envision the energy spiraling downward around you. With the finger of one hand, draw a spiral on the palm of your other hand starting from the center and going outward in a clockwise motion. As you draw on your palm, envision the electric blue light of Witch Fire being traced where your finger touches, then gently blow on your palm. Keep repeating this for about a minute or so and then switch hands and perform it on the opposite hand for a minute or so.

Exercise 31

Deep Feeling

Perform the Awakening the Hands exercise. Bring your awareness to your hands. Pay attention to the feeling of the muscles in your hand and the joints in your fingers. Note how they feel. Are they relaxed or tense? Now bring your attention to the skin of your hands; how does it feel? Does it feel dry? Moisturized? Now bring your awareness to the air against your skin and how it feels. What is the temperature? Is there a breeze or is the air still? Now return your attention to your muscles and joints. While holding this attention, bring your attention simultaneously to your skin and the air around it. Now go one step further and feel the energy around your hands by bringing your attention out beyond the air against your skin to the air that is not touching your skin but is around your hands. What does it feel like? Tingly? Prickly? Warm? Cold? Dense? Light? Keep repeating this until you get a palpable idea of what feeling energy with your hands feels like.

Exercise 32

Creating an Energy Orb

Perform the Awakening the Hands exercise. Rub your hands together for about thirty seconds, slowly decreasing speed and intentionally relaxing the muscles in your hands. Press your hands together as if they were in traditional prayer position, except turn your wrists so that your fingers are pointing outward directly in front of you. Slowly pull your hands apart, feeling the space in between them and visualizing a white ball of energy between them. This should feel a bit like static for most people, but everyone's perception is a bit different. Play with this energy, making the ball bigger and smaller. You'll notice as you try to press your hands together it will almost feel like magnets pushing each other away. When you're done playing with your energy orb, merely shake your hands as if you were drying them while envisioning the energy dispersing like the water you were shaking off.

Exercise 33

Psychometry

Perform the Awakening the Hands exercise followed by the Deep Feeling exercise. Run your receptive hand along your projective arm. Experiment with different distances between your hand and your arm. Can you feel a point where you start sensing energy? Try this with pets, plants, crystals, and other people. Visualize that this energy that you're feeling is a data stream full of information. While exploring the aura of your subject, intend to interpret the data stream. Clear your mind and physically touch the subject. What immediately comes to you? Is it a feeling, a thought, an image, an impression? Go with what comes to you immediately without overthinking it or forcing any information.

Clairaudience

Clairaudience is clear hearing. It's the ability to hear psychic information through auditory senses, whether internal or external. The most common form is internal clairaudience, which is internal dialogue in your mind. Sometimes the voice is your own, sometimes it's the voice of another, but there's a distinct feeling that it didn't come from your own natural thinking processes. Some will say that with clairaudience you'll never hear audible external voices unless you have a mental illness, usually schizophrenia or psychosis. Hearing external voices does not necessarily indicate that you have a mental health problem. As always, it's important to get checked if you're concerned—though questioning your sanity is usually considered a good sign of mental health.

Clairaudience undoubtedly can and does occur outside of your internal dialogue. So here are some of my rules to decide whether it's external clairvoyance or mental illness. (Again, please seek professional help if you have any concerns about your mental health.) If it's clairaudience, the voice will usually not be constant nor will the voice tell you to harm yourself or others, or degrade you. The most common experience of external clairaudience is a lot like hearing voices amidst running water or blowing wind, despite there not being any. External clairaudience is very short lived and not reoccurring. Most of the time it's more like overhearing a spirit or spirits having a conversation and what you pick up may not be decipherable, but much more like muffled voices. It's clearer if they're speaking directly to you and want you to hear them. Another common experience is indecipherable and often indescribable music, which I usually associate with the fae folk. Another common experience is hearing someone you know calling your name, and when you come to them, you find that they weren't calling you. I had this a lot as a child but not as much as an adult.

When developing clairaudience, it's normal to hear different pitches of ringing in the ears, similar to but different than tinnitus. This tends to be the opening stages of clairaudience when a spirit is trying to speak to you, but you haven't fully developed that ability yet. However, I have often experienced this ringing sensation when casting magick circles and found it to stop when the magick circle was released. But I assure you that I, and other very talented psychics, mystics, and mediums that I've known, have had external clairaudient experiences.

Exercise 34

Deep Listening

It's important to learn how to listen deeply to activate clairaudience. To do that you want to sensitize your ears to noise. We are exposed to so many sounds all the time that we ignore.

Get in a relaxed meditative state, close your eyes, and take a moment to listen. Try not to think about or label what you hear, just listen. What do you hear? Perhaps it's the television or music in another room. Maybe you'll hear your heater, air conditioner, or refrigerator running. Keep listening closely. Can you listen deeper and more clearly? How far can you hear? Perhaps you can hear the swaying of tree branches and bird song. What's going on outside of your home? What does the wind sound like outside? Can you hear the cars on the street or children playing? The key is to try to take in as much auditory information as possible.

Exercise 35

Homing In on Sounds and Creating Links

Let's hone the sensitization of your ears a bit more for stronger clairaudience. For this technique, either use headphones or listen to music that will be loud enough to engulf you without hurting your ears. I don't suggest performing this while driving as it's meant to be performed while in the alpha brainwave state. While it should be obvious, I want to stress that you should never alter your state of consciousness while driving. Driving requires full alertness, and remaining in beta is vital for safety.

For this exercise, skip all the previous steps in the Tuning In exercises and go straight to Entering Alpha. By this point you should have established a prompt to enter alpha instantly on command. Pick music that you enjoy but is a bit complicated. I like to use music by artists that involve instruments and effects that are unique and diverse in their range. For this reason, I tend to pick artists like Björk, Radiohead, Fever Ray, Nine Inch Nails, or the Anix. The reason being that these artists tend to use synths, sampling, and effects in their music that are unlike other artists, which for me makes this exercise more interesting, and widens my auditorial "palette" of sounds that my brain can use for clairaudience. However, it's okay to use any music that you enjoy.

Start the music and don't think about or dissect the music. Just like the Deep Listening exercise, you're going to want to take in all the music as a whole in a passive manner. When the song is over, pick one instrument from the song and start the track over again, focusing solely on that instrument. Tune in to just that single instrument without getting distracted by the other instruments or the vocals. For those of you who are more tech-savvy with music, don't isolate that instrument in a music editing program. The purpose is to train your ears and brain to home in on a single sound among competing sounds. Keep repeating this process, picking a different instrument each time.

Now let's build on this. Re-listen to the song as a whole passively as you did in the beginning. What color would the song be if it were a color? What would it taste like? What shape would it be? What would it feel like if it were a physical sensation? Where would you feel it in your body? What emotion would it be? As with all psychic phenomena, you want to build up cross-associations to have all of your abilities work in harmony together to relay as much information as possible and as clearly and vividly as possible. Now go back and re-listen to the song and home in on each instrument, determining what color, shape, texture, taste, scent, emotion, and area of the body it would be in relation to the whole song. Think of the song as a school of fish acting as a collective with its own signature, but each instrument as a single fish in that collective that has its unique individual characteristics.

When coming back to this practice to build this ability, make sure that you switch up the songs so that you aren't always performing this exercise with the same song. All right, now that we're done with all of this aural sensitization, deepening, and mental associations, we're ready to learn how to start building clairaudience for non-physical sources of sound.

Exercise 36

Creating Noise Associations

Now you should be at the point where you can start programming your mind to create associations between noise and other information. Just like the aura exercises earlier, you're going to want to start projecting an internal association out onto something external.

Do this by using your psychic prompt to get into alpha. Now let's start with yourself. How do you feel? If the feeling you had were a piece of music, what would the song be? If it was a sound effect, what would it sound like? Do this throughout your day and try to conjure that sound within your mind at that moment and associate it with the feeling. When you come across people, what music or sound would you give them in their current state?

As with the aura exercise, this will help you to create a link through neuroplasticity to extend your hearing from the normal range to clairaudience. If you end up hearing a sound that is different than the one you were trying to conjure, allow it to be so. This is most likely your Higher Self making corrections to your perception.

Exercise 37

Hearing Spirits

A *spirit ally* is a broad term for any spirit that has a working relationship with you that is beneficial. While the subjects of spirit contact and spirit allies are beyond the scope of this book, I feel it's important to discuss spirit guides briefly. Among the different types of spirit allies exists a specific type referred to as spirit guides. Spirit guides are spiritual beings assigned before incarnation by your Higher Self. Spirit guides are invested in your path and your personal development. Think of them along the lines of your invisible team of spiritual life coaches, mentors, and guides.

The length of time that a spirit guide works with you depends on different factors. Some are with you your whole life and are assigned to you before you're born. Some are only with you for a certain span of time or while you're working through or learning something on your path in life. Having a higher perspective, spirit guides are always in alignment with your True Will, a subject we'll explore later, whether you're conscious of that or not.

Choose a time and a reasonably quiet place where you will not be disturbed. Perform the Tuning In exercise. For this exercise, I recommend starting with spirit guides because they're a safe non-physical entity to begin working with. Mentally or verbally call out to your spirit guides to assist you in this exercise. You can simply say,

"I call upon my spirit guides to come and relay a beneficial message to me through clairaudience that will assist me on my path. Come gather close, friends."

It's okay if you don't have a super strong connection with your spirit guides yet; by acknowledging them you begin building that relationship. Visualize them coming close; you can simply envision figures composed of light coming close and surrounding you. Now focus on your breath and try to clear your mind of any chatter.

While in a relaxed, receptive state, pay attention to any inner dialogue or sounds that occur without trying to force it. Messages may be in your own internal voice or that of another. Simultaneously pay attention to your surroundings, just as you did in the Deep Listening exercise. You may find that you hear something external that's out of the ordinary; perhaps a dog barking, or a piece of music a neighbor is playing. Is there a message there for you? As you build this practice, you may find that you begin hearing external noise or dialogue that isn't coming from an external physical source. Don't forget that you can use the Psychic Dimmer technique to increase or decrease information. It is also helpful to modify that technique by imagining you have another dial that acts like a dial on a radio, where you can tune and adjust the frequency of noise that you are hearing.

Clairgustance and Clairalience

Clairalience is clear smelling. Clairgustance is clear tasting. In other words, psychic taste and psychic smell despite there being nothing to taste or smell. These are two of the rarer forms of psychic perception. While they are distinct, I group them together because taste and smell are so intricately linked as perceptions. These two psychic abilities tend to be more linked to interaction with spirits and mediumship, but aren't always. For example, I work closely with the deities Hekate and Janus. Each of them has a distinct aroma that I will smell when I know that they're engaging in contact or want to assure me that they are with me.

Interestingly enough these smells started with specific herbs and incense that I would burn for each of them as offerings, but there's also an additional smell added to each when I'm having a clairalient experience, even if I'm far away from their shrines in my home and haven't burned any offerings to them that day. I know when my grandfather is engaging in contact because there's a specific cologne, whiskey, and tobacco smell which will occur. Alternatively, certain smells have historically been associated with danger or malevolent energy such as the smell of sulfur.

Clairgustance is even rarer than clairalience. Sometimes clairgustance will give me specific information about a spirit, and usually as a form of validation in mediumship for the person I'm reading for. For example, tasting a particular food in my mouth can indicate a favorite dish the person loved or was known to make and is associated with. I may also taste or smell cigarettes and know that they were a smoker. However, sometimes the experience of clairgustance is just a psychic red or green light for me. For example, I tend to get a disgusting moldy taste in my mouth if someone or a spirit has vile energy. I also will get a metallic taste in my mouth if I'm being told not to trust the spirit or person despite evidence to the contrary; it tends to relay to me that the person or spirit has a hidden agenda. Through conscious eating and smelling and through conjuring those sensations, one can establish and develop clairgustance and clairalience.

Exercise 38

Awakening the Mouth and Nose

For this exercise pick a few different spices or essential oils and place them in different spoons or saucers and set them on a table. You may want a partner to help you with this as you'll be blindfolded. Enter into alpha and close your eyes. Smell each sample individually. Try to pick up on the subtle differences of each scent. How would you describe them? Does a specific color, texture, feeling, or sound come to mind when smelling it? Can you imagine what they would taste like if you were to eat them just based on smell? Go for a walk and pay attention to the scents you may typically miss. How do the flowers smell? The bakery? The air? The pavement? The soil? If you were to envision tasting them, how would they taste in your mouth? How would you describe the tastes? Just as with Deep Listening, you want to smell profoundly and intensely taste things. Make eating within your life a thoughtful process of just taking in the sensations of taste and smell and focusing on the nuances of these sensations.

Exercise 39

Conjuring Smell and Taste

For this exercise enter into an alpha meditative state. Think back to a smell that comforted you growing up. Think of a cologne or perfume that you associated with someone. Think of smells that repulse you. Think of what smells you associate with love. What scents do you associate with anger? What smells do you associate with depression? What smells do you associate with danger? What smells do you associate with safety? What aromas do you associate with anxiety? What scents do you associate with confidence? Go through each of these things and try to conjure the smell as actively as possible while focusing on the feeling or memory associated with it. Do this process with taste as well. If you are having a difficult time conjuring a specific taste or smell, try conjuring one and allow it to lead you to the other. For example, if I'm having a hard time associating a scent with comfort, but I know that the taste of my grandmother's pastries brings comfort, I would spend time focusing on what those pastries smell like.

Exercise 40

Creating Smell and Taste Associations

In the previous exercises, we started to pay attention to what we smell and taste and the emotional feeling that it aroused within us. As you go through your day and interact with people, ask yourself: *If their energy had a taste and a smell, what would it be?* Think back to different smells and tastes that you've associated with emotions. Project that onto them. Begin experimenting with your predictive abilities. When starting your day, ask yourself what the day is going to smell or taste like. At the end of the day compare how the day went with what you envisioned yourself smelling and tasting.

Chapter 5
PURIFICATION
AND SHIELDING

Cleansing yourself and your environment is usually one of the first things taught in books, along with shielding yourself before proceeding to psychic ability or magick. I have opted to ensure that you have some of the foundational practices down at this point so that your cleansings and your shieldings can be much more effective for you. Originally, I would teach it right off the bat but found that my students were struggling with effectively employing the techniques. By teaching them how to tune in and how to engage their clairs, I found a much higher success rate with their abilities to do so.

While there are many different techniques for cleansing, clearing, and shielding oneself using herbs, stones, and ritual tools, as psychic witches we want to be able to perform these tasks whenever we need to, and in some cases we don't have access to those materials. The lack of materials or tools should never prevent a witch from performing magick. In most cases, physical items serve as enhancements for the working that you are doing and while they have their place in magickal works, I firmly believe one should have the ability to perform magick at any time no matter their circumstances. That's why within this book there are no items or ingredients needed unless it's a specific ritual or spells that wouldn't be performed when you're out and about. Even then I strip the use of physical items to a bare minimum and use stuff that is readily available in any household.

Energy Cleansing

Remember the saying that "cleanliness is next to godliness"? In both magick and psychic workings, this is true. Cleansing the energy of a space and maintaining proper psychic hygiene of yourself and your area is crucial and something that I commonly find underrated in people's personal practices. Think about how you feel in a messy house with very little light. Now think about how you feel in a house that is clean, open, and full of natural light. One feels better, doesn't it? While there's a psychological component to feeling more comfortable in a clean space, I believe that's because we're picking up on cleaner energy, which makes us feel more at ease. When it comes to cleansing and shielding, visualization and willpower are critical components to empowering the cleansing.

I'm often asked how often one should engage in personal cleansing practices. My answer is "daily." Think of it like taking a shower. You wouldn't necessarily want to wait to be absolutely filthy before you decided to take a shower, right? Most likely not. You'd probably want to take a shower at least once a day to ensure that you don't get to the point of being filthy. This is particularly helpful when performing cleansings daily as you can work it into your regular hygiene routine. What about cleansing spaces? When it comes to maintaining a cleansed space (especially the place you're living and spending most of your time), you'll find that, just like physically cleaning, energetic cleansing is easier when performed in daily doses of maintenance instead of waiting for it to pile up until it's a monumental task. I usually do a full energetic cleansing of my house during new moons and try to keep up maintenance through smaller bits of cleansing daily.

Spiritual cleansing of self or space is almost always preceded by the physical cleaning. However, you can kill two birds with one stone and mix the two into one practice. For example, while taking a shower, envision yourself bathing in light and washing away energies that are clinging onto you that you don't want. When brushing your teeth envision yourself brushing away all the obstacles between you speaking your truth as well as any barriers between you communicating with others (including animals, plants, and spirits). While sweeping or vacuuming the floors, envision sweeping or sucking up stagnant energies within your home. For an extra boost, sprinkle a cleansing item—such as sea salt or cleansing herbs like rosemary, thyme, basil, or oregano, which are found in most kitchens—on the area that you are clearing. When cleaning surfaces in your house envision cleaning away sickness, sadness, anger, and other built up energies that are sticking to the atmosphere. You get the idea. Just tie a conscious meditative mental process behind the physical cleaning. Sunlight and fresh air also help greatly in cleansing a place—so open up those curtains and open up some windows to let some air circulate in.

Exercise 41

Psychic Purification

This is a much stronger version of the Psychic Cleanse exercise we already learned, but serves us better when we need a deeper level of cleansing so that we're purified of any energies that are extremely out of balance. The key to this is to engage each of your clairs while focusing your intention on cleansing and purifying yourself. In the exercise I will give ideas for each clair to engage, but feel free to replace any sounds, smells, visualizations, and so forth with those that you personally associate with a sense of cleansing and purification.

Tune in. Envision a beautiful prismatic light flowing all around you like a gentle but steady waterfall. The energy goes through your body as well as around you while washing out any energy that doesn't belong to you. While holding this vision in your mind, feel the light's warmth around your body and within your body, clearing your energy fields of anything that doesn't serve you. As you maintain this vision and feeling in your mind, begin conjuring up the sound of a heavenly angelic choir surrounding you from all directions and loosening and lifting up any blockages in your energetic body. Now let's engage the senses further by summoning up the smell of citrus and flowers filling the space that you're in and conjuring up a taste of spearmint in your mouth—smelling and tasting the cleansing occurring.

Exercise 42

Lifting Heavy Energies Out of a Place

Have you ever walked into a room and despite everyone smiling and putting on pleasantries you can feel that there was just some heated argument moments before you arrived? Heavy emotions and energies build up quickly in a space and can accumulate quickly, including where you live. The following exercise is one that I've led some of my fellow psychic witches in performing in Salem before we start our day of performing psychic readings. We do this because psychic readings can be heavily emotional and people can often bring in and leave their energetic gunk in a space. This exercise involves intoning a magickal formula with intention and physical movement.

The formula is IAO. This formula comes from Hermetic systems of magick such as the Golden Dawn. IAO represents three forces: Isis, which embodies the forces of nature and creation; Apophis, which embodies the forces of destruction and removal; and Osiris, which embodies the forces of resurrection and transmutation. Because of this, the formula is perfect for transmuting and lifting out heavy energies. With "I" we tune into the energies already there within the room. On "A" we are declaring the energy is being removed. Then with "O" we are shifting the room to a positive energy state.

The full intoning of IAO should be performed with one unbroken breath. Tune in. While standing, place your arms down at your sides with palms down to the ground. Take a deep breath and from deep within your belly begin intoning "I" (Eeeee). Feel it reverberating from the back of your mouth. As you intone turn your palms so that they're facing upward as if you're scooping the energy of the room upward and slowly begin lifting your hands, envisioning yourself raising the energy of the room. By the time your arms are parallel with the floor begin intoning "A" (Aaaaaah). Feel it reverberating in the middle of your mouth and notice your mouth opening a bit wider to make the sound. Keep lifting the energy up with your arms. Once your arms are above your head begin intoning "O" (Ooooooh). Feel it reverberating at the front of your mouth and notice how much wider your mouth is open to make the sound. Envision the energy fully lifting out of the space as you physically push it up through the room as far as your arms can reach. Perform this at least three times. You should notice a drastic shift in the energy in the space.

Protection

When you're working with energy, whether psychically or magickally, you begin to light up with that energy. That light attracts the attention of all sorts of entities. A while back I had asked a prominent psychic witch elder to come over and evaluate my home. I couldn't understand why so many spirits were being drawn to my home. Was I under psychic attack?

Upon driving over he said that he could sense that there weren't many magickal practitioners near me at all, due to the area I was living in. This is completely true, as the town I live in is predominantly populated with senior citizens and most (to my knowledge) are just ordinary folks without any interest in magick or psychic ability. He informed me that because of all the magick and energy work that I'm constantly performing in my home, my property was lighting up like a huge energetic beacon. Spirits of the area who aren't used to seeing people who are working with energy or magick were filled with extreme curiosity and thus were drawn to my house like moths to a flame, coming to investigate what was going on.

Not every entity that is going to be attracted to you is going to be benevolent, peaceful, or loving. Nor are they all going to be malicious. Be ever mindful that just as people range from dangerous to safe or beneficial to wanting to take advantage of you—spirits are the same in their diversity of personality and demeanor. This is one of the reasons why protection shouldn't be neglected.

It's also entirely possible to unintentionally curse yourself through your own paranoia of others cursing you. As we will explore soon, words and thoughts have monumental power for the psychic witch. Yes, there is always the possibility of others consciously cursing you, especially if you're out of the broom closet. People can also hurl curses unconsciously by directing negative thoughts and emotions—and therefore energy—toward you. However, there needs to be a balance between a witch's paranoia and natural precaution. Fixating on curses will only strengthen them, or even cause them if they're not there to begin with. If you are maintaining regular psychic hygiene and magickal protection, there's not too much to worry about. If you do have a curse, you can always refer to the technique to lift a curse in chapter 15.

A key to living with magickal protection is to have healthy boundaries within all areas of your life. Your inner world permeates out into the energetic world. By having firm boundaries with friends, family, coworkers, bosses, romantic partners, strangers, and yourself you are creating strong boundaries within your own aura. If you are letting people take advantage of you, doing things that you are resistant to, or engaging in behaviors that are bad for you, you are creating leaks in your aura. It's okay to have boundaries. You can tell someone "no" without having bad feelings toward them. You also never need to explain your boundaries once laid. A wise friend of mine often states that "no" is a complete sentence.

The Power of Language

When it comes to shielding, there's honestly nothing more powerful than living with integrity. What I mean by this is ensure that you're living an ethical life up to your standards. Most of this boils down to respect. Be respectful of other people, places, and spirits. By living a life of respect and integrity, there's less of a chance that other people or spirits will actively work against you since you're less likely to offend them. Walk your talk. Keep your word and speak with honesty. Think of speech as a magickal tool, because it is. We have magickal terms that are closely tied to the idea of language, such as *spells* and books of spells called *grimoires*, which is related to the word *grammar*.

"Abracadabra" is a famous ancient spell that folk etymologists believe is either based on Aramaic for "I create like the word" or Hebrew for "I will create as I speak." As you engage more and more in your development as a psychic witch, you will find that your words have power, even when you don't intend them to, and you will soon learn to exercise caution when speaking things out loud. There's a reason the message of many folktales and fairy tales is "be careful what you wish for" when engaging the magickal. By treating the power of language as a tool you can ensure you are keeping the power of speech sacred. By keeping your word you affirm to other people, spirits, and the Universe that your word is valuable and as such are more likely to create more allies than enemies. The more allies on your side, the stronger of a defense you will have.

However, this doesn't mean we should neglect shielding completely. That would just be negligent and naïve. Just because we are good drivers doesn't mean we shouldn't buckle up before we get in our cars. Likewise, just because we are good people who live with integrity and protect the power of our word doesn't mean that we shouldn't engage in psychic and magickal protection. Preventative magick is strong defensive magick. It's better to take precautions than not and have to deal with trying to fix the problems that occured due to neglecting our protection.

Exercise 43

Foundational Shielding and Protection

Now that we know how to cleanse our energy, this is the perfect time to learn how to shield ourselves. With shielding you want to feel completely secure and confident. We will explore a foundational practice of shielding and different ways to alter that shield to be appropriate for what you're doing. Sometimes you'll want a shield that completely stops the flow of any energy coming in and out, but this can also completely mute psychic perception. At other times you'll just want to filter out energy that is aggressive or negative, and this is usually my go-to when it comes to shielding. Figuring out which type of shield you need takes discernment, so trust your intuition. This foundational shielding should be a daily shielding practice; how you enhance it is up to your circumstances.

Tune in. Envision a brilliant white light a few feet above you. Verbally or mentally affirm:

"Spirit above me."

See it begin to descend as a column of light around your body, down to a few feet below you. Verbally or mentally affirm:

"Spirit below me."

The light comes up from below you and rises a few feet in front of you at chest level. Verbally or mentally affirm:

"Spirit before me."

See the light meet the point above your head where it started, where it then descends a few feet behind you at chest level. Verbally or mentally affirm:

"Spirit behind me."

The light moves counterclockwise until it is a few feet on your right. Verbally or mentally affirm:

"Spirit on my right side."

The light continues to move counterclockwise until it is a few feet on your left. Verbally or mentally affirm:

"Spirit on my left side."

It continues its counterclockwise movement until it reaches the point behind you again.

See all six points glow around you. The light begins to shine so brightly it forms a bubble around you. Verbally or mentally affirm:

"Spirit around me."

Visualize the glowing filling your body as if you were an empty vessel. Verbally or mentally affirm:

"Spirit within me."

Take a few moments to feel this light above, below, before, behind, on your right, on your left, outside, and within you. Then verbally or mentally affirm:

"Spirit protects me. Spirit blesses me. Spirit heals me. Spirit guides me. I am, I always have been, and I always will be One with Spirit."

Exercise 44

The Filter Shield

Perform the Foundational Shielding and Protection exercise. Take a moment to feel the white light all around you, strong and vibrant. Envision a silver filter forming around the outside of your aura. Visualize it like a mesh strainer made of pure silver light. You can let go of the imagery of the silver filter knowing that it's still there doing its job. Now repeat this process with a golden filter. Know that it will prevent negative energies from entering and allow energies that are positive to come through. You are not cut off from all the energies around you, but they will be filtered before they reach you and your energy field. State out loud or mentally:

"By lunar and solar
Opposites and polar
Energies that harm and wilter
Cannot pass my magick filter."

Exercise 45

Full Shields Up: The Elemental Fortress Technique

This form of shielding is best when you don't want to interact with the energy around you at all, but rather temporarily shut yourself off from any and all energy input around you. This means that energies cannot interact with you and you cannot interact with them while this shield is up. Know that with this shielding process, it will also be hard to perform magick. Think of this as a maximum shielding and putting yourself into energetic quarantine. Because of the strength of this shield, you'll want to be sure to take it down when you are done, and it's best to do a cleansing afterward. With this exercise you'll be psychically summoning the four elements of earth, air, fire, and water to help assist in this shielding and create a fortress around you.

Perform the Foundational Shielding and Protection exercise. Take a moment to feel the white light all around you, strong and vibrant. Envision the earth below you rising up to form an impenetrable brick wall all around you like a fortress. Next envision walls of fire outside of it, incinerating any energy that gets close to the walls. Outside of the wall of fire envision a moat encircling you with waves crashing violently for any energy that tries to get close to you. Outside of the moat envision a ring of cloud with strong winds blowing out of it, pushing back any energy that gets near it. Now envision the brick wall turning into a sphere made of brick surrounding you. Then envision the walls of fire turning into a sphere of fire, surrounding you. Follow this by envisioning the moat turning into a sphere of crashing waves around you, and finally envision the wall of clouds turning into a sphere of clouds blowing out strong wind in every direction.

When you are ready to take your shields down and are out of the dangerous environment, just perform the exercise in reverse. The sphere of clouds turns into the ring of clouds which evaporates. The sphere of waves turns into a moat again and then dries up. The sphere of fire turns into the walls of fire and then the embers die down until the fire has stopped. The brick sphere turns back into the brick fortress which then crumbles and returns back into the earth.

Exercise 46

Psychic Security System

You can shield your home exactly as you do yourself, substituting yourself in the previous exercises in this chapter with your home. Sometimes it's important to understand what is trying to invade the shields of your home so you can take care of the situation and ensure that someone or something isn't perpetually trying to invade your space. If something is more persistent than your shielding maintenance there's a realistic chance that eventually it will come through, whether it's a malicious spell, an unwanted spirit, or just general bad energies being sent your way. Because of this I've created a psychic security system within my home to alert me when unwanted energies are trespassing and to help me identify what it is.

Begin by tuning in. Stand in the center of your home. Begin to envision a grid of lasers surrounding your home creating a matrix. These lasers are a security system. When any energy tries to enter from outside in, the grid will psychically alert you in the same manner that a normal home security system would with an alarm sound and flashing lights. Now go room to room and focus on each wall, floor, and ceiling of that space containing the grid of lasers. Return to the center of your home and visualize the complete matrix of lasers as one cohesive system. Pick a wall in one room of the house and visualize a secret keyhole. Now focus on your psychic password (in the next exercise) as a key. With your willpower and intention insert the key into the keyhole and lock it. Know that nothing and no one can alter your grid without your password. State out loud:

"The password is fixed!"

Now go room to room and visualize a small silver globe the size of your fist at the top of the ceiling with an eye etched into it. These are your cameras. Anytime your security system is triggered it will take a psychic snapshot of what is trying to invade your home and will send it to you along with the alarm. If your alarm is going off and you're not detecting what it is, simply tune in and envision one of those silver globes before you and ask it to show you what it captured. It may show you information through one or multiple clairs. If you're unsure of the information you've received, go to a divination system such as tarot to double check the accuracy of the information you're picking up. It's important to remember that this exercise isn't a shield and can't block anything from entering; it's a detection system and not a defense system. So be sure to also have protection around your home.

Exercise 47

Psychic Password

A psychic password is exactly what it sounds like. It's a password that you create to lock and unlock certain things. While it's first being introduced with the Psychic Security System, it can be used in other ways too. The main idea is that it's an item which can fix or unfix the magick of something when the password is used. By "fix" I mean "to secure or fasten" and not "to repair." Saying something was "fixed" or "to fix" something in witchcraft means that the energy could not be altered once a spell was cast, and this was most often done with magickal tools.[10] With a password we are fixing energy but also leaving room for us to "unfix" the item as well, which is sometimes needed. It also ensures that no one else can mess with our shields other than us.

Tune in. Envision a key before you. Now you're going to program that key by engaging each psychic sense. Conjure up a sound, a physical feeling, an image, a taste, and a smell. Go through each one, one at a time. Now try to engage all of it at once, simultaneously hearing, feeling, seeing, tasting, and smelling the password. Envision your key glowing and becoming encoded with the password. To use your password on something envision a keyhole and use your key to lock and unlock the keyhole, thereby fixing or unfixing the energy.

While this technique is fairly simple and effective, you want to make sure that it's complex in its coding by picking clairs that don't normally go together. Here's an example password to give you an idea. The image of a pink flamingo, the sound of a car honking, the smell of clean laundry, the taste of lime, the feeling of tree bark against your hand. Notice how none of these things go together, which ensures that you won't accidently think of all of these things at once and that other psychics are going to have a harder time picking up every element of your password. Be sure to write down your password somewhere safe and secret like your Book of Shadows or a journal so that you can refer to it if you don't use it often.

---

10. Laurie Cabot, with Penny Cabot and Christopher Penczak, *Laurie Cabot's Book of Shadows* (Salem, NH: Copper Cauldron, 2015), 124.

Chapter 6
THE TRIPLE SOULS
OF THE WITCH

Unlike other mainstream religions and forms of spirituality, in witchcraft and many Pagan traditions, the soul is most often seen and worked with as plural and not singular. The most common division of the soul is three, though it can be more or less. The term *soul* is used to refer to the main aspects that compose a person's soul. These parts work together but also function independently and autonomously. They are part of a triad collective, but also completely separate. Essentially boiled down to the most basic understanding, the three souls can also be looked at as mind, body, and spirit. The term soul is often used in craft traditions to bring more reverence to these components and to discuss that they're more than their surface appearances.

These three souls are sometimes referred to in witchcraft as the "Three Souls," "Three Minds," "Three Selves," or "Three Walkers," though the division of the soul into three parts spans various other religious, shamanic, and spiritual traditions around the world. These three souls are considered to be the first aspects of our multidimensional biology and understanding them is beneficial for both magick and psychic ability. The primary influence in this ideology seems to come from the Faery (or Feri) Traditions of Witchcraft, which adopted it from Huna. The first time these were publicly written about within witchcraft was in Starhawk's *The Spiral Dance*, Starhawk herself being a former student of Victor Anderson's Feri Tradition.

The three souls are going to be referred to in this book in their most generic terms, which are the Higher Self, the Lower Self, and the Middle Self. The three souls have a focal point of access within the body referred to as the "Three

Cauldrons" within Pagan traditions. The Three Cauldrons are a concept deriving from the sixteenth-century sacred Irish poem called "The Cauldron of Poesy." It is believed that the poem refers to a secret Celtic oral teaching of three energy centers that has either been lost or carefully guarded. Each of these three soul components are ever present within a different level of reality: the three realms of the Witch's Tree, the three Celtic Realms, and the World Tree.

The Lower Self is the name used for our body and our primal, emotional aspects of ourselves. Humans are animals and this is the aspect of ourselves that is animal. The second soul is the Middle Self, which is a name used for our mind and is the aspect of ourselves that differentiates us from other animals. This is our human aspect. It's the part of ourselves that reasons, plans, analyzes and reminisces on the past. The final soul is the Higher Self, which is a name for the spirit. This is the part of ourselves that is the closest to divinity. Have you ever heard the phrase that we're spiritual beings having a human experience? Or perhaps you've heard that you don't have a soul, you are a soul with a body? These both refer to the Higher Self. It's the part of us that is eternal.

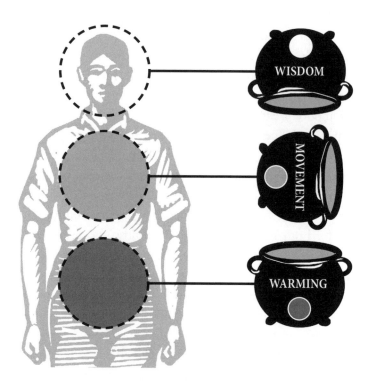

Figure 5: The Three Cauldrons of the Three Souls

Each soul aspect relates to various aspects of a witch's consciousness and therefore perceives different levels of reality. As such they have different levels of awareness, understanding, and experience. Each soul is tapped in to a different way of understanding energy and working with it. Therefore, by knowing each soul individually and through learning how to align them into one channel, one gains different perspectives of psychic information and different modes for the manipulation of energy. Through alignment of the three souls, one is fully present, fully engaged, and tapping in to all parts of their being, simultaneously.

Since each soul exists within a different realm, the witch also creates a crossroads when in alignment whereby the three realms merge as one. Each of the soul selves can also be seen as a kind of emissary of that realm and the entities that exist within it. As such, that soul-self has access to each of the four elements existing within that realm and resides within the element of spirit. Each of the realms has overarching elemental energy and sub-divided elements within them, and each soul has an alignment with that predominant energy. Water predominates in the Lower Self and the Underworld; the Middle Self and Middle World are mainly ruled by earth; and air mostly comprises the Higher Self and Upper World. Where these realms intersect and when the three souls are in alignment we have the element of fire.

Each soul can be understood a little better by exploring psychological models developed by Sigmund Freud and Carl Jung that relate to the three souls. Each soul is related to a specific symbolic animal energy that also helps us to relate and interact with these parts of ourselves. While each soul provides gifts of perception and energy work, they also come with their obstacles and challenges.

The Three Souls Before Birth and After Death

Each soul interacts and relates to reality before and after death, and they each have their own agendas to fulfill. The Higher Self wants to experience a physical reality for learning, experiencing, and growing. The Lower Self wants to elevate itself and heal its ancestral realm through incarnating. So the Higher Self descends while the Lower Self ascends and they form a contract. The Higher Self will provide a chance to elevate the Lower Self and allow it to ascend and heal past wounds, and the Lower Self will produce

UPPER

MIDDLE

LOWER

WORLD TREE

Figure 6: The World Tree

a body for the Higher Self to incarnate into. When this agreement is made they fuse and create the Middle Self, which is the individual personality that weaves together the Higher and Lower Self together as a single cohesive being.

Upon death, the Lower Self merges back with the ancestors and over time becomes more of a fluid collective entity than individual consciousness. If the Lower Self is rejected for some reason by the ancestors, meaning they find the incarnation's choices in life so objectionable that they refuse to allow that self to return to the Collective Consciousness, feeling there's absolutely no redeeming qualities that will enhance their pool collective and that there's nothing positive to contribute, the Lower Self becomes what is known as the immortal psychic vampire or a hungry ghost.

Since the Lower Self is continuously collecting life force from its connection to the land and environment, the rejected Lower Self is unable to do this without the shell of a physical body. Therefore, it seeks out those who are living to drain them of their life-force energy. These are intelligent parasitic beings and are usually what is described by non-psychics and witches as "demonic activity" or "poltergeists" looking to continually disrupt the lives of the living and induce states of fear, grief, and anger, which they feed upon. Likewise, most "poltergeist" or "demonic activity" can also be the psychic energy of the Lower Self of a living person lashing out uncontrollably, such as highly sensitive but emotionally and hormonally imbalanced teenagers going through puberty.

The Middle Self after death has a few options depending on what has happened to it. It can dissolve into the land, adding its experiences and wisdom into the earth; it can become a guardian of the land and retain a sense of its personality; or, if it is stuck for some reason and has trouble moving on or is rejected by the land, it becomes what we know as a bound spirit, or more commonly a ghost. The Higher Self never dies and is the only part of ourselves that is truly immortal. Being plugged into the Akashic Records as well as the Universal Mind of Collective Consciousness, it remembers all the experiences of the Middle Self and Lower Self incarnations. It's the part of ourselves that truly reincarnates, by moving to find another Lower Self to connect with and form a new Middle Self.

This is why mediumship, ancestral work, ghost hauntings, necromancy, and reincarnation can all be simultaneously true and coincide. The energies of each are different aspects of the soul. For example, a medium will usually deliver a spirit who has messages of healing and love, and while they will relay aspects of their Middle Self personality, it's more of an identifier with the person receiving the reading that they are in contact with the Higher Self of the person they knew in life. Those who work with ancestors and necromancy work are working with the Lower Selves. Those who are experiencing ghost hauntings are interacting with either rejected Middle or Lower Selves depending on the nature of the "haunting" as just mentioned.

It's the Higher Self that keeps directing the reincarnation process while paradoxically never leaving its connection with Source. The Higher Self records its experiences in the Akashic Records, which can be seen as the memory of the Collective. The Higher Self of every human is connected at a higher level, and at a higher consciousness. Our Higher Self has awareness of this unity of consciousness, which we might refer to as the Collective Consciousness. This also means that the Higher Self has access to all memories of life on earth and an understanding that these memories are also a part of its experiences, since the Higher Self understands that we are all unified at a deeper level. This is also why three hundred people can remember living as Cleopatra. The person who lived as Cleopatra, like all humans, was composed of more than one soul aspect, so her experiences have dissolved into different streams from which new lives have emerged. The new lives emerge with the possibility of having access to those memories of Cleopatra's life as a life they experienced as well. They have access to these memories because they're shared through the Higher Self. Another possible reason many people may share the memory of being a single person in a past life is because that person was an ancestor and they're sharing an ancestral genetic memory of that individual.

However, if these three souls can come into alignment and perfect the missions and form a new energetic container to bind all three parts, something entirely different happens. The three souls step off the cycle of birth, rebirth, forming, and dissolving. This is a state which in witchcraft we call the mighty dead, but which other traditions might call a saint, a bodhisattva, enlightened, godhood, or an ascended master. Soul alignment begins threading these three souls together in preparation of this state, but will not induce it. It's through fulfilling each of the souls' missions to perfection that one reaches this state of being. This is one of the primary goals of occultism and mysticism, and it is called apotheosis, which is becoming a god.

The Middle Self—The Default Consciousness

The Middle Self is the aspect of ourselves that can think, that has a sense of identity and a sense of other. The Middle Self has a perception of time and space as being linear. It allows us to make plans in the future, and to reminisce on the past. It's what enables us to translate information from the Higher and Lower Selves and convey it linearly and logically. It gives names and labels to objects, animals, people, and abstract concepts. It is the soul that understands language and communicates with other people, animals, aspects of nature, and spirits through the verbal, mental, and written word. It's what allows us to speak our reality as witches and to understand things deeply as mystics and occultists.

When a child is born, its Middle Self is created. At the moment of birth, it is imprinted with its astrological information and influences which affect and define its significant life lessons, strengths, and personality characteristics while incarnated. The Middle Self is who we are in spiritual evolution as humans right now.

When the Middle Self is out of balance on its own, we either are talking too much and not listening enough, or we are too quiet and not expressing ourselves enough. Therefore, it is the speaker and the listener. We may be unsure of or unable to speak our truth. On the other hand, we may be too locked into our dogmatic ideas of what the truth is, unable to look or think outside of the box or come to understand other points of views and beliefs. So, the struggles of the Middle Self on its own are certainty and uncertainty. It also may have problems with reconciling paradoxes, instead of allowing them to be.

When the Middle Self is out of alignment with the Higher Self, it can have difficulty perceiving others as parts of themselves and may have trouble connecting with concepts related to divinity. This can lead to existentialism, nihilism, or strict atheism (as opposed to a more agnostic atheism), whereby we are locked too much in a focus of mental faculties and unable to perceive higher spiritual energies or purposes. It can also be out of touch with its place of interconnection within the web of reality. We have a hard time seeing the forest for the trees. When out of alignment with the Lower Self, we can become stoic and disconnected from our feelings, relying on logic over emotion. We can become too practical and dismiss play, imagination, and indulgence in favor of prudence and practicality.

The closest psychological parallel that the Middle Self has is that of the ego. While the Middle Self isn't the ego itself, the ego is a part of the Middle Self and helps us understand what the Middle Self is. In modern spiritual teachings there's a bit of confusion surrounding the concept of the ego. Most condemn what they call "the ego" when they're really condemning "ego inflation," which is an exaggerated sense of self-importance, superiority, or arrogance. This has led to a bit of confusion around the use of the word ego in spirituality. There is absolutely nothing wrong with the ego as it's a sense of individuality, personality, and personal expression. However, the conflation with the ego and ego-inflation has been used by abusive spiritual teachers and cult leaders to have one abandon a sense of self for the purpose of dominating the individual. The ego is then diminished to the point of lack of self-worth and low self-esteem.

In witchcraft, we tend to not paint things with a broad brush when it comes to morality nor are we quick to lump things into a concept of "good" and "bad." A healthier division, from my perspective, is to discern whether something is in balance or out of balance. A balanced ego has a healthy sense of self-esteem and identity while an unbalanced ego always puts the self before others or, on the other hand, always puts others before the self. Finding a healthy balance of empowerment is important. In witchcraft a balanced use of power is having power with others and self, not having power over others or self.

The Middle Self's energetic anchor point is the heart area—or in witchcraft, the Cauldron of Motion. "The Cauldron of Poesy" indicates that the Cauldron of Motion is tipped on its side when we are born, able to receive the steam from the Cauldron of Warming of the Lower Self and the downpour of the waters of the Cauldron of Wisdom of the Higher Self. The Cauldron of Motion being on its side shows its neutral state. When we're optimistic about ourselves, our lives, the past, and the future it tips right side up, and it tilts completely upside down when we're pessimistic about these things.[11]

The Middle Self is represented by the animal imagery of the spider weaving together the Lower Self and the Higher Self into unison. It sits at the center of the vast web of reality, feeling the vibrations of movements in the higher and lower realms and interpreting its meaning and weaving bridges between them. The Middle Self is what creates threads of energy between ourselves and others through our interactions. It is the part of us which has relationships with others.

The Middle Self is connected to and exists primarily within the Middle World, which is our physical reality as well as its etheric counterpart. The Middle World also contains the liminal spaces and portals between different worlds. In the World Tree, it is the trunk of the tree, the part that we interact with the most easily, and that seems to be on the earth itself. Elementally the Middle Self and the Middle Realm is represented by the element of earth (which is not to be confused with physical earth or the planet Earth) and corresponds to the Celtic realm of land.

Exercise 48

The Web of Interconnection

The Web of Interconnection is a method that I use to connect with people over distances. In my personal psychic practice, I often don't interact with my clients at all. I just need to know their name, location, and age or astrological sign to perform the reading. People often ask how I can read people if they're not in front of me. The simple answer is that we're all entangled energetically and we're all connected. It's merely about focusing on this connection to tap in to it.

For this exercise and the next, a good way to find subjects to test this on is to ask friends for info from their friends (with the subject's permission) who aren't your mutual friend. You can also pair up with people that you know online. If you don't know anyone online that's interested in participat-

---

11. Christopher Penczak, *The Three Rays: Power, Love and Wisdom in the Garden of the Gods* (Salem, NH: Copper Cauldron Publishing, 2010), 61–67.

ing, you can visit my website (www.MatAuryn.com), where I have community groups set up to meet and practice with other psychic witches.

Tune in. Think of a person to whom you wish to connect with psychically. Remember to have their permission to connect with them. Visualize an amber sphere of light glowing at your heart center. Say the full name of your target along with any other identifying information three times out loud. Usually, I say the name, location, and age if I have it. Sometimes I don't have or want to ask someone's age so I will often ask for their astrological sun sign. So for example, you would repeat something like this:

"Jane Doe, Seattle, Washington, Libra. Jane Doe, Seattle, Washington, Libra. Jane Doe, Seattle, Washington, Libra."

As you repeat the information of your psychic target, speak it as if you're giving commands to your amber sphere of light to seek this person out.

Visualize the amber sphere shooting out from your heart and into the cosmos before you. As it leaves you, it leaves behind it a gossamer web of gold energy like a spider. The amber sphere is seeking out your target and will connect with it no matter how far the distance, and will connect with their heart center, creating a psychic cord of feeling between the two of you.

Once the connection has been established, you are now connected heart to heart, and you're ready to perform a psychic reading over any distance. If the person is a stranger to you, try tuning in to what they look like physically. Don't force it, just visualize the outline of a person and allow your mind to start filling in characteristics such as hair, eyes, skin tone, body shape, etc. It's okay if you don't know what they look like. Allow their image to unfold within your Witch Eye. When you're done with the reading, mentally retract the amber light. Perform a psychic cleanse, call back your energy, and ground.

Exercise 49

≈

Performing a Health Scan

Healing is a skillset long associated with witchcraft. Witches were among the first energy healers, herbalists, midwives, and nurses. Before modern medicine, those who needed healing would go to a witch, a shaman, or another healer who had a connection to plants and the spirits. It's believed that early humans were able to discern which plants killed and which plants healed through observation of animals, trial and error, and through information provided by spirits or the spirit of the plant itself. The word *pharmacy* comes from the Greek word *pharmakeīā,* meaning the use of drugs and medicine as we understand it today, but also the use of sorcery, spells, charms, curing, and witchcraft. In witchcraft, we see healing as holistic, something that isn't purely the physical body but incorporates every form of well-being possible to bring balance and wholeness to the person who needs healing. We can see a bit of a comparison with many indigenous cultures whose word for healing and magick is often translated to the English word *medicine*.

To heal, we need to know what we're healing first, though. To do this, witches use many different techniques to discover what may be wrong with the individual. One of the simplest but most effective ways is to scan a person's energy. While training under Laurie Cabot, one of the exercises she has us do are health scans. Just like with the Web of Interconnection exercise, all we have to work with is the name of a person and their age and location, nothing more. We use the techniques taught to us to try to psychically diagnose this individual who has already been diagnosed by a medical physician so that the other person can verify the results.

I have a strong aversion to gore and even the human body. I joke that I like to pretend that underneath our skin is nothing but energy and light. For some reason organs and blood and veins and bones make me queasy. As a psychic there are many times that people will ask you health questions. Never use health scans alone. They should not be the sole method of diagnosing illness. If you or someone you know has health concerns, they should schedule an appointment with a health care professional. The health scan should be seen as only complementary to any other conventional medical diagnoses. If you're reading for someone else, you should really stress this and inform them clearly that this is not a diagnosis.

During one of my health cases, I saw red wine (as opposed to blood) with white chunks in it. I then saw a Valentine's Day heart with those white chunks around it as well. I interpreted this as saying there's a problem with blood pressure and cholesterol that's affecting the heart. This turned out to be correct.

In another health case, I kept seeing a pair of balloons next to each other inflating and deflating. That's because the problem was with their lungs. If I had seen the lungs and the ailment, I would've been grossed out and thrown out of my altered state. So I received the information in a way that I could handle. But I naturally wouldn't interpret that as saying "I feel like your balloons aren't filling up right." Ha! However, during another health case study, at one point I felt pain in my head and kept seeing an impact. I said, "I feel like they were in a car accident because I keep getting blunt trauma to the head, which has caused brain damage." This turned an accurate hit (pain on the head from the impact that caused brain damage) to being profoundly incorrect by interpreting it as a car accident. The following is an adaption of what I've learned from Laurie Cabot.

Tune in. Perform the Web of Interconnection exercise. Once connected, begin to focus on the subject's physical image. Reach your hands out as if they are right in front of you. Begin to feel their facial features with your hands, and run your hands over the surface of the double of their body in your Witch Eye, scanning them several times. Pay careful attention to any area that keeps drawing your attention. Visualize the image turning into an X-ray that can see inside of them, and that can zoom in and zoom out. What do you see?

Pay attention to any feelings that you're feeling within your own body including discomforts, pains, or aches. Hold your thumb and pointer finger out as if you're holding an empty vial in your hands. Physically and in your Witch Eye use the vial to scoop up a sample of their blood.

Hold this vial up to your Witch Eye and shake it up. What do you see? Is the blood dark or light? Does it have white spots or dark spots? Does it swish around like it's thick or thin? Don't be shy and say whatever you're seeing and feeling. At this point if they are open to it you can send them healing energy, which we will explore later in this book.

Exercise 50

Memory Magick

During a podcast interview I was asked how I have the ability to retain all the information that I read in so many books and how I read so quickly. This is a technique that I've created, based on some of the previous techniques, that allows you to not only record information but also be able to access it through your memories. This has also helped me out in gaining access to email accounts that were over a decade old that I couldn't remember the passwords to. This technique can be helpful when studying or performing any sort of test.

Hold your psychic prompt as taught in exercise 18. The key here is to enter into alpha on command and achieve that relaxed state. In your Witch Eye, simply imagine a record and stop button on the screen of your mind. Envision this button being pushed to tell your mind that you want to retain information that you're reading or listening to. That's all there is to it!

To access information that you can't remember, simply hold your psychic prompt again and enter into a light meditative state. imagine a search engine bar on the screen of your mind and envision yourself entering in the information or memories you're looking for. Relax and allow your mind to gently search for the information until it comes to you. Try not to force this. This can take a few minutes up to a few days based on how deeply buried the memories are and how important the brain has marked it to remember. Intentionally recording information with your psychic prompt makes this information easier to access.

The Power of Inquiry

"To me, the question mark (?) is the most sacred symbol of the witch. For we dare to ask the heretical questions," writes southern conjurer, witchcraft elder, and faery seer Orion Foxwood.[12] This is a compelling statement. When I was a child, I was raised in a very religious household. I remember my inquisitiveness got me in a lot of trouble at Sunday school but it also opened up a whole avenue of exploration outside of the church's grasp. Questioning theological and philosophical holes in what we were taught was greatly frowned upon. After all, the serpent in the garden was the first creature ever to ask questions leading to Adam and Eve eating from the Tree of Knowledge. Surely, those types of questions came from heretical thinking. At least that's why my elders in the church assured me.

---

12. Orion Foxwood, footnote to "The Witch Lives" in *The Flame in the Cauldron: A Book of Old-Style Witchery* (San Francisco: Weiser Books, 2015), xix.

For example, I was taught three things that were contradictory. The first was that God is omniscient and knows everything about the past, present, and future. The second was that God was all-loving. The third was that God sent those to eternal suffering who turned away from his commandments. Meditating on these made me uneasy. I asked, "Why would God send us to suffer for all eternity if he was all-loving?" I was told that it was because we were given free will by God to choose that path. This was incorrect, as technically the serpent gave humanity free will. "Yes, but if God is omniscient and he knows what we're going to choose before he even creates us, why would he create us knowing that we freely chose to go against his commandments and have us suffer for all eternity? If he truly loved us, wouldn't he either not create us or end our existence instead of torturing us for all eternity?"

Those questions didn't go over well, and I was punished when I went home after my Sunday school teacher had a chat with my guardians. I remember the words my Sunday school teacher used to try to silence my questions, which only made me question deeper: "Who are we to question God?" She rhetorically and dismissively asked me. For me, this was a brilliant question. Who are we? Who is God? Why are we? Why is God? These were questions that boggled my mind and began a thirst for understanding that has not been quenched to this day.

Questions are more important than answers. The power of questions and critical contemplation are a driving force behind the development of civilization. Questions have been the singular most important aspect of human existence. I can only imagine our far ancestors asking questions such as why do plants grow, how can I stay warm, why are we here, where did we come from? I cannot help but see inquiry as the driving force behind science, philosophy, religion, and all innovation in history.

Questions have the power to inspire, illuminate, stimulate, create, or destroy. If we want to take on the great mysteries and grow as individuals, witches, and psychics—we must ask questions. Questioning is the only way that witchcraft will ever evolve in the future, as inquiry is the predecessor of all great shifts in progress. Our Middle Self has the power of intellect and the power to truly explore our Universe around us through critical thinking and questioning. When teaching witchcraft and psychic ability I always encourage questions, not only to ensure that everyone is grasping what I'm sharing but because I usually learn something myself or discover a question I hadn't contemplated yet.

Exercise 51

Contemplative Inquiry

For this exercise, you don't need to tune in or meditate in any formal way. Instead, you're going to be working solely with your Middle Self using your mind to discover the root of who your Middle Self is. You're just going to be having an internal conversation with yourself and continually asking yourself a repetitive one-word question in response to your initial questions. Those questions are "who?", "what?", "where?", "when?", "why?", and "how?" You want to keep this dialogue up until you can't answer your questions anymore. This conversational inquiry will give you insight into who you are as an individual, what your motives are, clarity on unconscious conditioning, and insight into what you truly believe. It can be beneficial to write your results in a journal and track your progress over time.

Example Initial Questions:

Who am I?

What is divinity?

What am I?

What is consciousness?

What is holding me back from following my dreams?

What do I believe?

Why do I have this desire?

Why do I exist?

Why does anything exist?

Where am I?

Why do I think this?

Why do I act this way?

Why am I feeling this way?

How am I holding myself back?

Why do I treat myself this way?

Why do I treat others this way?

Why do I want to enhance my psychic ability?

Why do I want to perform magick?

What is my real motive?

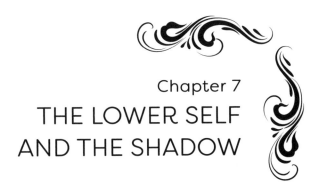

Chapter 7

THE LOWER SELF
AND THE SHADOW

The Lower Self is the aspect of yourself that feels and is connected to our physical, emotional, and energetic environment. It is primal consciousness. Because it has a perception of time and space as always here and now, it holds on to emotions and energies from the past and experiences them as if they're occurring now. Some traditions of witchcraft call this soul the "Sticky One" and I think that's a very apt description. It implies that it acts as a sponge, absorbing and taking in everything from its environment, but also that it is the messiest soul in some regards. The Lower Self is pre-verbal and communicates much like a child who hasn't learned to speak yet, or an animal companion trying to relay information. It speaks through feelings, cravings, and desires.

The Lower Self is often described as being animalistic, primal, child-like, instinctual, and sexual. Being primarily composed of blood and flesh, the Lower Self comes from the ancestors, and the ancestors live through us in what witches such as Raven Grimassi refer to as the River of Blood, the unbroken lineage from our first ancestor to now.[13] As such their wisdom flows through us in the form of evolutionary instinct and ancestral knowledge, and we are in tune with their guidance and help if we're open to it. Upon death, we return this favor when the Lower Self merges back with the ancestors with the knowledge and healing accumulated from that incarnation—

---

13. Raven Grimassi, *Communing with the Ancestors: Your Spirit Guides, Bloodline Allies, and the Cycle of Reincarnation* (Newburyport, MA: Weiser Books, 2016), xxi.

which is why the ancestors choose to join with the Higher Self to begin with. The Lower Self is where we come from in the spiritual evolution of humanity. It is our ancestry and our ancestral gift.

When it comes to psychic ability, the Lower Self assesses its environment and relays that information to the Middle Self, which interprets the bodily sensations, emotional feelings, instincts, gut feelings, and hunches into thoughts and words. When the Lower Self and Middle Self are in alignment they have a conversation, which we call intuition. We intuit information about ourselves, others, situations, environments, and possible paths without knowing logically why.

The closest psychological parallel that the Lower Self has is the id. While the Lower Self isn't the id itself, the id is a part of the Lower Self and helps us understand what the Lower Self is. The id is the impulsive, primitive, aggressive, sexual part of ourselves that consists of all the things we've inherited biologically from our parents. A newborn child is all id, and later develops an ego, and a superego—just as the progression of the evolution of the human soul consists of the Lower Self as being where we came from, the Middle Self being where we are, and the Higher Self being where we are going. The id seeks pleasure and induces anxiety to avoid unpleasant feelings and pain.

The Inner Child

The Lower Self can also be understood as the Inner Child, and as such loves to play and have pleasurable experiences. Earlier when we explored imagination and psychic immersion, we were tapping in to our Inner Child and our Lower Self. The Lower Self is the part of us that dreams and imagines and is entirely non-logical, and thereby not constrained by it. The Lower Self connects with the Higher Self the easiest in this manner, and the Middle Self weaves them together to make sense of the information. This is why intuition, which is a Lower Self phenomenon, and psychic ability, which is a Higher Self phenomenon, tend to blur together and weave in and out of each other.

When the Lower Self is out of balance on its own, we're either indulging ourselves too much, lacking restraint, and becoming prone to addictions and bad habits, or on the other hand denying ourselves pleasurable experiences and (in the worst cases) denying our body what it craves for survival. Discipline is the challenge of the Lower Self, and finding out what the appropriate level of control is to make us content while simultaneously not giving into our vices and ultimately destroying our lives. Freud compared the id to a horse, and the ego to the rider, so one way to look at the Lower Self's challenge is as training a wild horse without abusing it.

When the Lower Self is out of balance with the Middle Self, we become unconscious of our feelings and our experiences, and deny the wholeness of who we are, thus creating shadow issues. The experiences, emotions, and aspects of ourselves that we don't want to own or acknowledge are shoved from the Middle Self, but the Lower Self always has an awareness of them. In analytical psychology, they call this the shadow and refer to the collection of these experiences and identities as the Shadow Self. The Shadow Self is what the ego rejects from the light of its consciousness and is pushed back into the shadows of the mind where it isn't being looked at but is still there. The Shadow Self, however, is still a part of ourselves and the more we ignore it, the more it acts up to try to get our attention and come back into the light of our conscious mind. This is expressed as unconscious action and projections onto others. Another challenge of the Lower Self being out of alignment with the Middle Self is that we may become too naïve and gullible, thus lacking discernment and critical thinking.

When the Lower Self is out of alignment with the Higher Self, we become monsters, being the worst examples of humanity. The Higher Self has a spiritual moral compass of right and wrong. In a sense, when the Lower Self is out of alignment with the Higher Self we become too feral, quicker to damage and harm others in a fight-or-flight behavior. We may also have a hard time relating to and empathizing with others or caring about how we affect the environment and animals. This can also lead to energetic and emotional vampirism behavior, where we manipulate and drain other people consciously or unconsciously to feed our energy supplies.

The energetic anchor point for the Lower Self is the belly area—or in witchcraft, the Cauldron of Warming. The Lower Self as the Sticky One accumulates life-force energy from around us to fuel us, and "The Cauldron of Poesy" indicates that the Cauldron of Warming is right side up when we're born, sending the steam of its lifeforce up to the Cauldron of Motion and warming it up—hence its name. The Lower Self is represented by the animal imagery of the serpent rising in healing and wisdom, an image that appears in many cultures from Kundalini to the staff of Asclepius, the caduceus of Hermes, the staff of Moses, and the uraeus of Egyptian pharaohs. Just like the serpent, the Lower Self is close to the earth, always connected and a part of the natural world and the physical body.

The Lower Self is connected to and exists primarily within the Lower World, which is the realm of the ancestors, initiation, healing, regeneration, and wisdom. In the World Tree, it is the roots of the tree that are unseen diving deep into the Underworld. Elementally the Lower Self and the Underworld Realm are represented by the element of water, which represents emotion and astral energies and corresponds to the Celtic realm of sea.

The Shadow Self

Swiss psychiatrist and psychoanalyst Carl Jung was a prolific man whose work was highly influential not only in the fields of psychology and psychiatry but also addiction recovery, alchemy, archeology, art therapy, anthropology, dance therapy, philosophy, spirituality, religious studies, and the paranormal; he even influenced spiritual interpretations of quantum mechanics. Many of his concepts have had a considerable influence on Paganism and witchcraft as well, such as his concept of synchronicity, archetypes, and the Shadow Self.

Carl Jung's theory of the Shadow Self is that we all carry parts of ourselves within our psyche that we want to disown. If we think of our ego as being the light in which we see ourselves, the Shadow Self is everything that resides within the psyche that the ego is rejecting.[14] Though comprised of our shame and self-perceived weaknesses, the Shadow Self isn't necessarily wholly negative either; it can also be aspects of ourselves that we aren't owning or addressing. For example, if someone has low self-esteem, their sense of empowerment is residing within their Shadow Self as compensation, because they're refusing that aspect of themselves in how they view themselves. To address the Shadow Self is to take an honest look at ourselves through introspection.

---

14. Carl G. Jung, *The Collected Works of C.G. Jung: Volume 9, Part II, AION: Researches Into the Phenomenology of the Self* (Princeton, NJ: Princeton University Press, 1959), 8–9.

On the ancient temple of the Greek god Apollo in Delphi were inscribed the words "know thyself." This temple was known throughout the world for the Pythia, which was a title for the high priestess of this temple who would give prophecy as an oracle to Apollo, who among many things was a god of prophecy himself. The Pythia was one of the most famous psychics and trance channelers in all of recorded history and was revered for her accuracy in ancient times. The inscription on the temple obviously held a high level of importance for the temple, and these words give us a critical insight into an important aspect of this great psychic—the importance of knowing and mastering oneself thoroughly. To do so, we need to understand who we truly are and not just who we want to believe ourselves to be.

Jung proposed that one becomes enlightened about one's nature by not only focusing on the positive aspects of ourselves and our spirituality but by also confronting our own Shadow Self.[15] Like a child who is ignored, the more one refuses to confront their Shadow Self, the more it throws tantrums to get us to acknowledge it. The most common method of our own Shadow Self trying to get our attention is to project it upon other people and to try to battle it externally, which only perpetuates the problem of disowning our Shadow Self instead of acknowledging and integrating it healthily.[16]

But why is dealing with our Shadow Self essential to psychic ability or witchcraft? One reason is so that we are aware of what we're projecting onto others and what we are genuinely picking up psychically, and being able to discern the difference. Devin Hunter also teaches that many less friendly spirits will often try to use our fears and vulnerabilities against us.[17] This can range from hyper-inflated or diminished self-esteem to our deepest fears, addictions, and vices. By being clear about who we are and reassigning our Shadow Self into more balanced and beneficial roles, we are sitting on the throne of sovereignty in regard to our psychic ability and our witchcraft. This means that we are in control—not our Shadow Self and not external

---

15. Carl G. Jung, *The Collected Works of C. G. Jung: Volume 13: Alchemical Studies* (Princeton, NJ: Princeton University Press, 1983), 265–266.

16. Carl G. Jung, *The Collected Works of C. G. Jung: Volume 13: Alchemical Studies* (Princeton, NJ: Princeton University Press, 1983), 297.

17. Devin Hunter, *The Witch's Book of Spirits* (Woodbury, MN: Llewellyn Publications, 2017), 83–84.

spirits—and we are centered in our personal power. As witches, all of the components that make up ourselves are constantly manifesting our reality— Higher, Lower, and Middle Self. We want to be in as much control as possible of our manifestations; as such, we need to make sure that our Shadow Self is manifesting in alignment with our other parts and not sabotaging our will.

In the Feri Tradition of Witchcraft, the Shadow Self is seen as an externalized projection of ourselves that is sometimes referred to as the Shadow Lover or the Shadow Twin.[18] The Shadow Lover is an aspect of our Lower Self. Witchcraft is a crooked path between seemingly different polarities and is also a path of alchemical purification, of taking these opposite aspects and unifying them into wholeness. This alchemical union of two different parts is an important motif in many witchcraft traditions. Whether it's the masculine and feminine divine coming together in the Great Rite,[19] or the God of Light and the Horned God coming together to battle each other throughout the year on sabbats,[20] or the divine twins as serpent and dove merging together as the Blue God,[21] the focus is on the merging of opposites.

The Kybalion, an esoteric text that discusses the principles of the nature of reality, points out two important things to keep in mind here. The first, which *The Kybalion* refers to as the Principle of Polarity, is that everything has a polar opposite. There is light and darkness. Male and female. Hot and cold. But the idea of polarity can only fully be understood through the next principle, which is the Principle of Rhythm. The Principle of Rhythm states that everything is a spectrum between the two poles that are constantly in flux. Gender is a spectrum, as is light and darkness, and temperature.

Both Jung and many occult traditions place an emphasis on combining opposites into wholeness. Jung refers to this idea as individuation, which

18. Storm Faerywolf, *Forbidden Mysteries of Faery Witchcraft* (Woodbury, MN: Llewellyn Publications, 2018), 29.
19. Raven Grimassi, *Encyclopedia of Wicca & Witchcraft* (St. Paul, MN: Llewellyn Publications, 2003), 193.
20. Christopher Penczak, *The Outer Temple of Witchcraft: Circles, Spells and Rituals* (Woodbury, MN: Llewellyn Publications, 2014), 372.
21. Storm Faerywolf, *Betwixt and Between: Exploring the Faery Tradition of Witchcraft* (Woodbury, MN: Llewellyn Publications, 2017), 29–30.

is acknowledging the aspects of ourselves that we are unconscious of and integrating them into our sense of self. In alchemy, this is referred to as the Great Work and in occult traditions (including many witchcraft traditions), Baphomet is a symbol of that Great Work. One of my teachers refers to Baphomet as "the Great Initiator." Baphomet is a symbolic image created by occultist Éliphas Lévi which was based on the trials of the Knights Templars in the fourteenth century.

The image may appear frightening at first, but I believe that's part of the intention. The image, contrary to popular belief, is not an image of the devil, but rather an image of the Universe as a force and intelligence and a portrayal of the Greek god Pan,[22] whose name was compared by ancient Greeks with the word *pan*, which means "all." Lévi writes that the image of Baphomet is the key to all magic as it is the source of all magical energy, which he and many occultists of his time referred to as "astral light."[23]

Baphomet is the image of all the forces of the Universe combined into one symbolic entity. Baphomet is male and female, light and dark, all the classical elements, animal and man, above and below, angel and demon. On Baphomet's upraised arm is the word *solve*, an alchemical term for breaking down of elements; on his lowered arm is the word *coagula*, which is an alchemical term for uniting elements together. It is the source from which all things come and to which all things return, just as the traditional prayer in the Feri Tradition states: "Holy Mother! In you we live, move, and have our being. From you all things emerge and unto you all things return."[24] *The Wiccan Charge of the Goddess* written by Doreen Valiente states similarly, "For I am the Soul of Nature, who giveth life to the Universe; from me all things proceed, and unto me must all things return." In *The Golden Dawn*, the phrase "O Soul of Nature, giving life and energy to the Universe. From thee all things do proceed. Unto Thee all must return" is recited in ritual.[25] Both Gerald Gardner and Aleister Crowley state that Pan is the all-devourer and

---

22. Éliphas Lévi, *Transcendental Magic* (York Beach, ME: Weiser Books, 2001), 308.

23. Éliphas Lévi, *Transcendental Magic* (York Beach, ME: Weiser Books, 2001), 104.

24. Storm Faerywolf, *Betwixt and Between: Exploring the Faery Tradition of Witchcraft* (Woodbury, MN: Llewellyn Publications, 2017), 22–33.

25. Israel Regardie, *The Golden Dawn: A Complete Course in Practical Ceremonial Magic* (St. Paul, MN: Llewellyn Publications, 2003), 433.

Figure 7: Baphomet

all-begetter.[26] They are all referencing the same divine force that is embodied within the image of Baphomet.

Victor Anderson is quoted as saying "God is self and self is God and God is a person like myself."[27] Similarly, in Aleister Crowley's Gnostic Mass, the line "there is no part of me that is not of the gods" is spoken.[28] For me this suggests the Hermetic axiom "As above, so below. As within, so without," as well as the idea of a holographic Universe, wherein we are fractals of the larger structure, containing within us everything of the larger structure. We are not only a part of the Universe, but we are also a microcosm of the Universe itself. We are not only a part of Baphomet, but we are also Baphomet ourselves. Therefore, our work is the Great Work of the Universe, to know ourselves in all parts, which is a key to magickal and psychic connection and mastery.

Self-Possession

Self-possession is what it sounds like: being fully embodied and in alignment with one or more of your souls. If we think of our body as a building, we can choose to treat it like a haunted house with unknown aspects of ourselves roaming around freely and creating chaos, or we can treat it as a divine temple, honoring and having a personal relationship with the aspects of ourselves that dwell there. We gain this relationship through invoking or summoning that aspect of ourselves to know ourselves better, align ourselves with that aspect, and build a relationship through which we harness its energy.

Exercise 52

Self-Possession: Invoking the Lower Self

The Lower Self can be invoked for healing, shape-shifting, glamour, communing with animals, plants, the natural world, and nature spirits. The Lower

---

26. Gerald Gardner, *The Meaning of Witchcraft* (York Beach, ME: Weiser Books, 2004), 161; Aleister Crowley, *The Book of Thoth* (York Beach, ME: Weiser Books, 2004), 62.

27. T. Thorn Coyle, *Evolutionary Witchcraft* (New York, NY: Tarcher/Penguin, 2004), 43.

28. Lon Milo DuQuette, *The Magick of Aleister Crowley: A Handbook of the Rituals of Thelema* (York Beach, ME: Weiser Books, 2003), 241.

Self can be invoked for ecstatic rituals and practices, astral journeying, dream recall, and to tune in to your intuitive self when you need to access your environment or a situation from a more fight-or-flight mentality. I also invoke the Lower Self when I need to commune with my Inner Child or Shadow Self for healing or self-care.

Begin by tuning in. Bring your awareness to your lower cauldron. Take a deep breath, envisioning yourself sponging up all the energy around you, and fill your lower cauldron with this energy. See it as an offering to your Lower Self. Take another deep breath and call upon your Lower Self to overshadow you, visualizing yourself being surrounded by your own protective primordial Shadow Self.

"Primal Self, Sticky One, Made of Shadow and Dust,
The Shape-Shifter, Fetch-Maker, Carnal One of Lust,
The Undefiled, Wild Child, Dancer on the Ledge,
Baneful Healer, Fire Stealer, Rider of the Hedge,
Pleasure Seeker, Dream Speaker, Open-Hearted Hands,
Nonverbal, Eternal, Ancestral Link to the Land,
I call you forth to rise up now as a sacred part of me!
I call you forth to rise up now and overshadow me!"

To return back to your normal Middle Self state of being just perform the Closing Down exercises.

Exercise 53

Dialoguing with the Shadow Self

Sarah Lynne Bowman, PhD, first introduced me to the work of Carl Jung and the concept of the Shadow Self. Sarah is a scholar, author, professor, and immensely spiritual human being. The following is a ritual that she developed based in part upon the divine feminine meditations of Jumana Sophia from Her Mystery School, as well as the pioneering work of Carl Jung and William Glasser.

This is a ritual she's provided to help seekers get in touch with their Shadow Self aspects, by coming into alignment, establishing a dialogue, transmuting, and integrating them. The goal of this ritual is to help individuals remove shame from their shadow aspects, identify them as allies, uncover the core needs within them, and figure out how best to integrate and balance the Shadow Self into their daily lives. Thus, this practice views the integration of the Shadow Self as an important way to promote psychological and spiritual well-being. I suggest performing the invocation of the Lower Self before beginning this ritual.

Find a place to get completely comfortable, yet remain alert and undisturbed. Sit or lie down as needed.

Take several deep breaths. On the in breath, focus on calling your energy back to yourself from all of the distractions in the world, resting in your core. On the out breath, soften back into your spine, allowing it to support you without effort.

When you feel like your energy has returned to your core, take a scan of your emotional self. What are you feeling? Are you peaceful? Do you feel any disruptions, such as anxiety, fear, anger, agitation? Notice these emotions and where they reside in your body without any need to change them.

If you have a particular shadow aspect with which you would like to work, bring it to mind. You may find that aspect residing in your emotional body already, manifesting as anxiety, anger, or fear. Or, you may feel emotions arise as you contemplate a specific shadow aspect, such as greed, seduction, wrath, self-pity, and so on. Simply notice at this stage what feelings come up for you.

When we access our shadow elements, we often feel shame, fear, or judgment around them. Take a few deep, cleansing breaths. On the in breath, imagine where the shame, fear, or judgment is located in your body. Is it focused on a particular energy center? Focus your attention on that area on the in breath. On the out breath, imagine the shame, fear, or judgment releasing, like a loose ribbon unraveling into the Universe around you. Repeat this exercise until you feel the block removed.

Next, imagine the shadow aspect. When you envision it, what does it look like? Does it have a color, a texture, a symbol? Does it become embodied as a person or animal? Hold the image in your mind.

Now, you will give that shadow aspect a voice and a name. The name can be a word or description. The Shadow Self tries to communicate with us in all sorts of ways that we may not recognize, mostly subtly or indirectly. The goal here is to come into direct dialogue with the Shadow Self and communicate, asking it what it wants and why.

Dialogue with your shadow aspect. What need is your Shadow Self trying to fulfill? Some basic needs might be power, security, fun, belonging, or freedom. Or, your need might be more specific and unique to you. Imagine your Shadow Self wrapped in mystery, like a shell wreathed in smoke. Open the shell. What need is inside the shell that is core to you? What does it look like? What color, shape, or texture is it?

Discuss with the shadow some ways in which it has been trying to get that need met. Have these ways caused disruptions in your life? Have they harmed others in some way? Have you repressed this shadow aspect altogether, suppressing the need? Do you often claim not to have the need at all? Have you attempted to address the need in another way in your conscious life, one that has not quite fulfilled you? Explore how this shadow element manifests in your life.

Discuss with the Shadow Self ways in which you could get that need met that can benefit yourself and others. If you have a need for a certain type of fun, how can you have fun more safely? If you have a need for power, how can you empower yourself while also empowering those around you? Ask your Shadow Self to become your ally in your journey. Collaborate. If your Shadow Self suggests behavior that you find unethical, be gentle in explaining why you do not wish to pursue that energy or action. Be helpful in creating alternative suggestions. Find ways to give your Shadow Self what it needs.

Imagine yourself showing a gesture of gratitude and love to your shadow aspect. Perhaps you give your Shadow Self a hug. Perhaps you imagine light energy holding hands with shadow energy. Express love and gratitude for your Shadow Self and all the lessons it has to teach you, while coming into balance with it. Remember that your Shadow Self is your ally and always has been.

Thank your Shadow Self and release it. Take several breaths to return back to yourself. Thank yourself for having the courage to undergo this journey.

Take out your journal and write down your experience. What did your shadow dialogue teach you? Did you come to any conclusions with your

Shadow Self as how to best express its energy? What did it feel like to release your shame around your Shadow Self? Notice any emotional or energetic shifts and log them in your journal.

I suggest titration when undergoing this exercise. In other words, address each shadow element one by one, or even piece by piece of the larger complexity of the aspect. I do not advise attempting to unearth all of the aspects of the Shadow Self at once, which may overwhelm you. Rather, work slowly and individually with each aspect and learn the lessons contained within it. You may choose to continue to work with these aspects over the course of several sessions or even years. The Shadow Self will evolve and manifest in new ways as you continue your own growth. Remain attuned to its mysteries, own and integrate it, and you will come more into balance with yourself.

Exercise 54

Lower Self Glamour Spell

Glamoury is a magickal working that changes how something or someone is perceived. The word comes from the Scottish word *glamer* meaning magick, spell, charm, or enchantment. It is believed to be a corruption of the English word *grammar*, which has similar occult connotations behind its meaning. In the mid-1800s the word lost its magickal meaning and was associated with someone attractive, appealing, and seductive, much like the word "bewitching." In Celtic folklore, glamoury was most often associated with the fae folk who would appear to shape-shift and change how things appeared, such as making straw look like gold. Glamoury isn't about physically changing shape of a person or object, but rather creating an illusion that convinces the senses that something is different than it is in actuality. When I think of glamoury, I think of octopi. The octopus is able to camouflage itself to almost any environment, and some species of octopi, such as the mimic octopus, will contort their bodies to mimic other sea creatures to fool both predators and prey. In worst-case scenarios, if the octopus needs to, it will also release a cloud of ink to confuse the predator and make a quick escape, much like a stage magician disappearing with a smoke bomb. This spell is a temporary glamour. I have found that it works for about a day if well cast. The idea is to have your Lower Self project an image around you to others who will pick it up through their own Lower Selves, though unconscious of it. In this sense, it's very much communicating the illusion through animal instinct from one person to another, which is then interpreted in the conscious mind similarly to intuition, where they just perceive something about you without being consciously sure why. I have used this in job interviews to be perceived as the perfect employee. I have also used this when speaking in front of large crowds when I need to feel much more confident than I'm feeling at that moment. The uses are countless.

For this spell, stand in front of a mirror. Begin by invoking your Lower Self. See the shadowy haze of your Lower Self surround you like the ink of an octopus, distorting your image. Hold the image of how you want to be perceived in your Witch Eye. If you want to come across as more confident, what does that look like? What would a confident version of you look like? If you want to come across as more attractive, what does that look like? Really focus on that image and stare at your reflection without blinking. You should notice that your image begins to fade away slowly. Keep holding on to that image of how you want to be perceived and overlay it onto your image in the mirror. Then recite:

"By this glamour I perform,
I shape and shift my own form,
Like the octopus within the sea,
Creating illusion so all others agree,
That all of their senses do perceive,
Myself as this image I now conceive."

Exercise 55

Telepathy with Animals and Small Children

As discussed, the Lower Self isn't all shadow, it's also the animal and child aspects of ourselves, which just happen to be two areas that most people are disconnected from or have disowned. Most people push these aspects of themselves into their shadow. My dad is one of the most magickal and psychic human beings I've ever come across, though he'd never use those words himself.

My father in many ways reminds me of an animal whisperer as a male biker equivalent. He's always had this ability to connect with really small children and with animals. It really has to be seen to be fully appreciated. Both animals and children just have this natural ease with him and seem to fully understand what he's conveying to them. As a child, he would be able to summon pigeons and then would train them. He's able to get the angriest dogs to calm down and be friendly. Children also absolutely adore him, and not just because he's starting to look like Santa Claus with a long white beard as he ages.

This used to really baffle me, especially since, as I said, my dad is a Harley-Davidson-riding biker, and however you're envisioning that is probably close to how he looks. I didn't understand why someone who could be so intimidating-looking could have animals and children understand he wasn't a threat at all. That is, I didn't understand until I started studying the three souls more and realized that this connection he has with small animals and small children is because my dad is fully in alignment with his Lower Self and thus is able to communicate on that nonverbal level with them. Since animals and very small children are nonverbal, connecting with the Lower Self is the best way of connecting with them.

My family also tells me stories of when I was an infant. My father would come into my room to my crib and touch my forehead and I would start bursting into laughter. With time he would just point at me and I would start going into hysterics. Eventually, my father would be in another room of the house and would point in my direction through walls and I would begin laughing, which became a favorite "trick" of his to show people whenever they came to the house.

Begin by tuning in and invoking your Lower Self. Feel your animal nature or your childlike nature based on whom you're communicating with. Make sure that you're feeling completely relaxed and calm. The key here is to not only exude the energy that you want to convey but to literally transfer it to them. You want to keep in mind what type of animal you're working with or the age of the child. For example, a dog's idea of friendliness may differ from a snake's. Conjure up a feeling such as friendliness, love, playfulness, or calmness.

While doing this, hold in your Witch Eye an image of some sort that's related to what you want to convey. For example, if it's a cat, hold on to the image of gently petting and feeding the cat while it purrs. If it's a child perhaps hold the image of making a silly face and the child laughing. Take these feelings and images and imagine them as external, coming out of your energy field and being placed in the recipient's field. Experiment with all the other clair-senses as well. Try playing with taste, smell, touch, sight, and sound and sending that. Likewise, in this state of consciousness be open to what you're perceiving by engaging your own ESP. You may very well find that they are also sending you information.

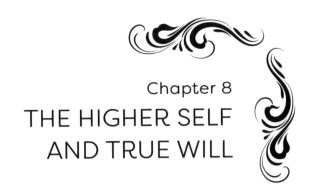

Chapter 8
THE HIGHER SELF
AND TRUE WILL

he Higher Self is our divine consciousness. It's an aspect of yourself that has never left divinity. It has been referred to as the Personal God, the Holy Spirit, Holy Soul, or the Holy Daemon (which is a Greek term for spirit, not a demon in the popular sense). It is the part of us that is perfect, eternal, and consistent through each lifetime. It is beyond time and space and isn't linear at all. It is one with the whole Universe, and its full nature is slightly beyond our scope of complete understanding. The Higher Self is aware of all of our incarnations and oversees our experiences in those incarnations.

The Higher Self is usually referred to as that spark within us, but it is most often perceived as a spark above our heads and not directly located within the body itself. It's literally higher than our physical bodies. Before I knew about the Higher Self, I had this experience where I woke up one night and in a hypnogogic state saw a white glowing orb hovering about a few feet above my face. It was a beautiful pearlescent white globe about the size of a cantaloupe. This orb was beaming a white light upon my face, and I just had this acute sense that this light was myself somehow. Later when I learned about the Higher Self, this made much more sense to me.

As mentioned earlier, before we incarnate, the Higher Self is looking to have specific human experiences and also to fulfill a role in its interaction with other Higher Selves. The Higher Self connects with the stream of ancestors and creates a contract. The ancestors provide the physical vessel of a body, and the Higher Self delivers the spirit. They unite together to form the Middle Self of personality. This is paralleled in alchemy where three elements are emphasized—Mercury, Sulfur, and Salt. Alchemy is greatly misunderstood as being literal instead of the exploration of spirituality and experimenting with transmuting the self. In alchemy Salt is born from the union of Sulfur and Mercury, two elements that are seen as opposite combined into one.[29] Among these many layers of meaning and association with these elements, we also understand that Sulfur refers to the Higher Self, Mercury to the Lower Self, and Salt to the Middle Self.[30] So again, Higher Self mixed with Lower Self creates the Middle Self.

As mentioned, the Higher Self is looking to have learning experiences to add to its knowledge to evolve itself. This knowledge was called the Akashic Records by some mystics such as the Theosophists and Edgar Cayce. Mainly, it's the memories and records of every experience of every incarnation that the Higher Self has had. The Higher Self is always in contact with the Akashic Records, since it's part of the consciousness of the Higher Self itself, and all the Akashic Records are part of the Divine Mind and Collective Consciousness' memory. And just as the Lower Self relays intuitive information that it's picking up on an instinctual level to the Middle Self based on information of its surroundings, the Higher Self conveys information of a psychic nature to your Middle Self, meaning when the two are communicating information is gained that couldn't be gained by other means, often transcending space and time.

The Higher Self's energetic anchor point is the crown of the head—or in witchcraft, the Cauldron of Wisdom. "The Cauldron of Poesy" indicates that the Cauldron of Wisdom is upside down when we are born, empty and unaware of our divine nature. I see this state as the wisdom of the Higher Self splashing against the underside of the cauldron which is facing upward, spraying outside of ourselves and not hitting the middle Cauldron of Motion. When we come into alignment with our Higher Self, the Cauldron of Wisdom is turned right side up, and the wisdom of the Higher Self fills

29. Dennis William Hauck, *The Complete Idiot's Guide to Alchemy* (New York, NY: Alpha Books, 2008), 99–100.

30. Christopher Penczak, *The Three Rays: Power, Love and Wisdom in the Garden of the Gods* (Salem, NH: Copper Cauldron Publishing, 2010), 63.

the cauldron and overflows like a fountain into the Cauldron of Motion of the Middle Self.

The animal imagery of birds—frequently a dove or an owl—often represents the Higher Self, swooping down in flight from the heavens to the earth, as it is not from this world at all but rather from the divine cosmos which is its home. The Higher Self is connected to the Upper World, which is the abode of the Divine Mind, the Collective Unconscious, and the realms of cosmic and divine forces. In the World Tree, it is the branches of the tree reaching upward to the sky. Elementally the Higher Self is that of air and corresponds to the Celtic realm of sky. The idea of air and breath and spirit are linked almost universally as the "breath of life," and even the word "spirit" comes from the Latin word *spiritus* which translates as "breath." Similarly, the word for spirit in Hebrew is *ruach*, which translates to "wind"; in Sanskrit the word *prana* is the word used for life force and translates as "breath."

True Will: Our Divine Purpose

The role and mission that the Higher Self is looking to fulfill is its purpose of incarnating onto the planet. This higher purpose—the desire of the Higher Self—is often referred to as the True Will, meaning the primary drive of the Higher Self for this incarnation. Occultist Aleister Crowley coined the term True Will. Being in alignment with your True Will doesn't mean that life will be easy or free of conflict, and not everyone will discover or fulfill their True Will in a lifetime. Your True Will is not one singular thing to accomplish, but I think it's better to think of it as a journey instead of a destination. Being in alignment with your Higher Self is like having a compass that will help direct you along that journey. To come to know our True Will, we must transcend the ego and the Middle Self's desires. Crowley referred to the desires and wishes of the ego and external motivations as the "lust of results" and stated that True Will should be fulfilled without resistance or the lust of results.

When we are in alignment with our Higher Self, we begin to have direction in life and are fulfilling our True Will. True Will is the conversation between Spirit and the Higher Self. The Higher Self speaks through synchronicity, symbolism, and revelations. We come to know the nature of our True Will through aligning with the Higher Self. When you are in alignment with your Higher Self, you can express and experience Divine Love and divine grace—or in the terminology of witchcraft, "perfect love and perfect trust." We experience deep states of peace, harmony, and union with other people.

The closest psychological parallels that the Higher Self has would be a combination of Freud's theory of the superego and Carl Jung's theory of the Collective Unconscious. While the Higher Self isn't the superego or Collective itself, these are aspects of the Higher Self that help us to understand what the Higher Self is. The superego is composed of two primary aspects, an ideal self (a perfected sense of ego) and a conscience. The superego tries to control the id's impulses and behaviors that are out of alignment with the superego's sense of morality; it may relay feelings of pride for embodying our morals and may cause a sense of guilt for disregarding our morals.

The superego is always striving to be the ideal versions of ourselves when it comes to being a "good person." While I am not entirely of the mind that the superego's conscience or striving to be the perfected ideal version of a righteous person accurately embodies the Higher Self, I think if we replace these with the idea of always attempting to embody our True Will and for our ego and id to come into alignment of the superego, we are closer to the essence of the Higher Self's nature. The Collective Unconscious is the part of our consciousness which is not formed by experience and is a universal transcendental knowledge which all people are tapped into, albeit unconsciously, that can be likened to the Akashic Records and the Divine Mind.

Going back to the earlier metaphor provided by Freud of the Lower Self being a wild horse that the Middle Self is training, we have a similar metaphor being used in Plato's *Phaedrus*, in which he refers to the soul as made up of three parts: a charioteer, and two winged horses.[31] The charioteer, like in our earlier analogy, is the Middle Self, the conscious aspect of us trying to direct two very different aspects of ourselves. One horse is completely of divine origin. This parallels with our idea of the Higher Self. This winged horse wants to assist us in flying directly into the abode of the gods and the path of enlightenment, as is the nature of True Will. The second horse, though, is partially a normal horse of earth and as such has earthly desires and appe-

---

31. Plato, *Phaedrus*, edited by R. Hackforth (Cambridge: Cambridge University Press, 1972), 69–77.

tites, and can be unruly and stubborn, which fits great with our notion of the Lower Self. When the two horses and the charioteer are not in alignment they have difficulty moving in any one clear direction, because their will isn't unified. The Higher Self knows exactly where we should be going, but cannot get there unless the rest of our parts are working in alignment.

Witchcraft as a Priesthood

It's through alignment with the Higher Self that one is able to better understand and commune with deity and higher spirits in whatever form that they may experience it. Many witches are also priests and priestesses of different gods and spirits, while others may just be focused on being a priest of their Higher Self. Regardless of what spirits or deities a priest or priestess serves, they are first and foremost servants of humanity, since every human is divine. By servant, I don't mean a slave or any connotation that brings up, but rather that priesthood is a path of service. A priest or priestess guides, directs, and counsels others. A priest or priestess of the Craft holds the door open to seekers just as the door was opened for them. A priest or priestess holds the space for healing. A priest or priestess helps point others in the right direction without telling them what to do.

A priest or priestess of the Craft differs from priests and priestesses of other religions and traditions in the sense that the mission is to lift other souls up instead of holding sway and dominance over them. A priest or priestess of the Craft empowers and helps others find their own path to healing and connection with the Divine, instead of dictating dogma to those they are serving. In fact, most priests and priestesses of the Craft don't agree 100 percent with one another. This is bound to happen when there's no central authority when it comes to witchcraft; everyone has a different relationship and connection to magick, and everyone has a different True Will. Fiction writer Terry Pratchett hilariously wrote, "Some people think 'coven' is a word for a group of witches, and it's true that's what the dictionary says. But the real word for a group of witches is 'an argument.'"[32] If you interact with the larger Pagan or witchcraft community, you're bound to find strongly opinionated people arguing about their points of views and

---

32. Terry Prachett, *Wintersmith* (New York, NY: HarperCollins, 2006), 94.

beliefs. A priest or priestess of the Craft is also a bridge, a bridge acting as an intermediary of the gods and spirits and humanity to create good relations and connections with one another for the highest good.

In my perspective, a priest of the Craft walks the crooked path between the left-hand path of personal power, sovereignty, and self-service, and the right-hand path of healing, serving others, and empowering others. It means that the witch is sovereign as an authority of his or her own spirituality, not an authority over the spirituality of others nor has another jurisdiction regarding personal gnosis of another. It is likely that you will come across the terms "high priest" or "high priestess" in witchcraft too, and that has different meanings based on which tradition of witchcraft that individual follows.

When studying in the Temple of Witchcraft, I had a conversation with Christopher Penczak, who was my mentor at the time. He explained that the most fundamental difference between the two is that a priest or priestess of the Craft is one who conducts rituals and develops magickal skills for a personal relationship with deities, powers, energies, and spirits; they are ultimately responsible for their own reality and self. A high priest or high priestess, on the other hand, takes the role of working with others, and takes responsibility for a part of the greater whole. Also traditionally, a high priest or high priestess is the priest or priestess in service of other priests and priestesses that are learning and working under that high priest's or high priestess's tradition.

Does being a priest or priestess mean that witchcraft is a religion? No. Witchcraft is not inherently a religion, though it can be for some. Witchcraft is more of a spirituality, or rather how one relates to the world of spirit, and that's going to be unique and individual for each witch. Witchcraft can also be religious in some cases depending on how you interpret the word religion. For example, in the tradition I'm in, the Sacred Fires Tradition of Witchcraft, I view the higher levels of it as a religion in the sense that the priests and priestesses all have a common language, understanding, and interaction with the gods of our tradition on a mutual level of understanding despite our individual personal experiences when alone. We approach the gods and the mysteries in a prescribed way so that we're all on the same page and same wavelength as each other when working together as a group. By having a common theological, philosophical, and cosmological model that we share, one could see this as a religious model. We also view ourselves as ministers of the gods and goddesses of our tradition, acting as intermediaries between them and our people.

Exercise 56

Self-Possession: Invoking the Higher Self

The Higher Self can be invoked to learn your mission, life purpose, and True Will within this lifetime, and to commune with deities and angelic entities. I invoke my Higher Self when I'm feeling lost and need divine guidance in life. The Higher Self can also be aligned with for purposes of growth and development as a witch, psychic, and human being. The Higher Self can also be invoked when you're dealing with entities or situations that are dangerous and you need a stronger authoritative power. The more you come to know your Higher Self and learn to embody it, the more authority you will have over unbalanced energies and entities. Energy tends to want to adjust to other energies that are more dominant or prevalent in the area, as energy seeks to conform in resonance with other energy. A high vibrational and balanced resonance will either make lower energy flee or balance it out in harmony.

Begin by tuning in. Bring your awareness to your upper cauldron. Keep breathing, and focus your attention on a spark of prismatic and opalescent white flame refracting all the colors of the rainbow within its whiteness just above your head. This is your Higher Self, the indestructible holy aspect of your divinity. It begins to pour down into your upper cauldron, filling it and overflowing the cauldron, pouring all around and within you. Solidify the experience with the invocation of the Higher Self by saying:

> *"Higher Self, the Holy One, Made of Light and Breath,*
> *Divine Spark, Bornless One, Never Knowing Death,*
> *Seraphic Soul, Angelic Role, Shining in the Heavens,*
> *Ascended One, Enlightened One, Master of Quintessence,*
> *The Unconfined, Mastermind, Bestower of My True Will,*
> *Who Understands, Hidden Hand, the Mover of the Mill.*
> *I call you forth to descend now as a holy part of me!*
> *I call you forth to descend now, overlighting me!"*

To return back to your normal Middle Self consciousness, just perform the Closing Down exercises.

Synchronicity

Synchronicity is a concept coined by Carl Jung which he defined as a meaningful phenomenon whereby a link between two events without a cause-and-effect explanation appears to be coincidental on the surface, yet holds great significance.[33] Jung believed that the Universe, through the Collective Unconscious, was constantly trying to talk to us through synchronicity. Both psychics and witches know that the Universe is not random but instead has patterns, cycles, structure, and most of all, meaning.

An example of synchronicity was several years back when I was living in California. At the time I was working with my father in his plumbing business. One night I had an intense experience with a spirit who took the form of an owl. The experience was so surreal yet vivid that I wondered whether I had had a dream of experiencing an owl spirit or if it had been some sort of creation of my own imagination. The next day as we approached the first client's door I noticed that the doormat was an owl. I thought that was an interesting coincidence.

However, as the day unfolded every single house that we went to had either an owl statue, doormat, wind chime, sign, or some other representation of an owl. I was pretty amazed and realized that this was a sign from the Universe that the experience was real. While thinking about how strange it was that every single house had an owl of some sort, I came back to my apartment and there was an advertisement flyer on my door with an illustration of an owl. Over the years, that spirit has been my closest spiritual contact and ally.

As psychic witches, it's important to be aware of and open to moments of synchronicity. It's equally important to not consciously force synchronistic meaning in things. For example, there are many people who believe that 11:11 is a sign from above, which perhaps it may be. However, I've also seen that a lot of folks who believe this are constantly looking for 11:11. Around 11:00 a.m. or 11:00 p.m. they'll start repetitively looking at their watches

---

33. Eugene Pascal, *Jung to Live By: A Guide to the Practical Application of Jungian Principles for Everyday Life* (New York, NY: Warner Books, 1992), 201.

until it's 11:11 and then take that as some sort of sign. Synchronicity is more spontaneous and unexpected than actively seeking out patterns where there may not be any.

Exercise 57

True Will Synchronicity Meditation

In this guided meditation, you will be meeting with your Higher Self to receive a symbol that it will use in your daily life through synchronicity to show you if you are in alignment with your True Will, and a symbol to show you when you are straying greatly from it.

Tune in. Invoke your Higher Self. Close your eyes and envision that a heavy fog begins filling the area. The fog begins obscuring everything around you. The fog fades and you find that you're standing in front of a castle. Take a moment to really take in what the castle looks like to you. What material is it made out of? What does it look like? The castle is strikingly beautiful and vaguely familiar, though you can't place it. You know that whoever owns this castle is a powerful individual.

You step forward toward the enormous castle doors. As you approach the doors they begin to swing open, inviting you to step inside. Inside the castle, you enter a great hall with beautiful and enormous stained glass windows on every wall leaking in colored light everywhere. There's a regal red carpet leading to the back of the hall and at the end is a magnificent throne. High above the throne is a mirror suspended in the air and covered in silk cloth. Down around the throne are entities composed of light. These are your spirit allies and guides, some that may be known to you and some that are not.

You approach the throne and sit upon it.

The throne is comfortable and thrums with power. Slowly the throne begins to levitate with you upon it. You rise higher and higher until you're positioned directly in front of the silk-covered mirror that is suspended in the air. As you look at the mirror, the silk cloth lifts off the mirror. You gaze into the mirror and see your reflection, but instead of seeing the face you're accustomed to, you see the reflection of your Higher Self in its image. Take a moment to see how your Higher Self is presenting itself to you at this time.

You ask the reflection of your Higher Self to give you a symbol to show you when you are in alignment with the path of your True Will. The reflection on the mirror shifts and changes and you are shown a symbol. What is it? This is the symbol that your Higher Self will communicate to you through synchronicity in your daily life that you are on the correct path.

You thank your Higher Self and ask for a symbol to show you that you have strayed greatly from your True Will. Once again the mirror shifts and changes and you are shown another symbol. Take a moment to observe this symbol. It is a warning sign that your Higher Self will show you through synchronicity in your daily life that you are straying far from your True Will. Thank your Higher Self for this symbol. As you do, the silk cloth covers the mirror and you find yourself upon your throne descending back down to the ground.

Stand up and walk back down the regal red carpet and out the doors of the castle. Once more a fog begins swirling around you obscuring everything in sight and you find yourself back where you began this meditation. Open your eyes and write down your experiences in your journal.

Exercise 58

Spell to Transmute Blockages toward True Will

In this spell, we're using sympathetic magick (sometimes also called imitative magick). Sympathetic magick is when you're using spell items to metaphorically represent something else. Sympathetic magick is one of the oldest magickal practices, and some believe that an example of it goes as far back as early man painting images of successful hunting on cave walls to ensure a bountiful hunt.

For this spell, all you will need is a small bowl, a small tea light candle, and about four ice cubes. In this spell, we're using the ice to represents the blockages in your life that are preventing you from being in alignment with your True Will. The tea light represents you and the light will represent your Higher Self's intervention to not just remove the obstacles and blockages but to transmute that energy to assist you in coming into alignment with your path. All energy can be transmuted according to the Hermetic Principle of Vibration, which states that all energy has the potential and ability to be changed.

Tune in. Invoke your Higher Self. Place the tea light in the center of the bowl. Place the four ice cubes in the bowl to surround the tea light.

Focus on the divine light around yourself from your Higher Self invocation. Firmly speak:

"I light this candle with the power of my Higher Self."

Light the candle, feeling the over-lighting of your Higher Self infusing the flame. Feeling the divine authority of your Higher Self hold your hands over the bowl with the tea light and ice cubes and firmly state:

"As the light melts the ice, the magick begins,
Transmutes blockages without and within,
Assists me in rising above to now fulfill,
The divine unfolding of my holy True Will."

As the ice melts, the tea light should rise higher and higher up until it's being supported by all those previous blockages. When the ice is melted remove the tea light and dispose of it. Pour the water onto soil so that the earth may gain nourishment from it and break down and transmute those blockages even further.

Exercise 59

∽

Universal Unity

This meditation will help strengthen your spiritual powers by connecting you more strongly with everything in the Universe, and helping you to learn to identify and relate with it. This will enable your psychic powers to flow more easily as you realize there's a common aspect that you share with everyone and everything. It will help you with your magick as you understand your interconnection with everything else as self and your ability to alter it as you would your body. Think of this exercise as a great workout to help build all those spiritual muscles to be strong and effective.

Tune in. Invoke your Higher Self. Close your eyes and focus on the prismatic white light above your head that is over-lighting your physical body. Focus on everything within the light of your Higher Self's halo. Your Higher Self is a part of Source. All of you is a part of that Source as well: your body, your emotions, and your thoughts. Take a moment to open to the Divine Love of Source, a feeling of unconditional love for existing, a love without judgment but just for being. Mentally think to yourself, "This is me and I am that—powerful, divine, and united in love."

Feel the Divine Love strengthen the Higher Self's over-lighting halo. The light grows brighter and encompasses an area beyond your body—five feet in every direction. Repeat the process of mentally taking in all that exists within everything the light touches and repeat to yourself, "This is me and I am that—powerful, divine, and united in love." Keep repeating this process extending your light more and more in every direction in larger and larger increments while reciting the affirmation. Keep expanding it until it's lighting your entire space, your country, your continent, the planet, the solar system, the galaxy, the Universe, and so on for as long as you can imagine. When it's reached the farthest reaches you can possibly fathom of reality, feel the light withdraw back to its normal glow around your body. When you are ready, open your eyes.

Chapter 9
FLAMES OF THE WITCH'S SOULS

Why is working with the three souls important for psychic or magickal ability? By working with the Three Soul model we're given different lenses from which to view reality. Think of it as having a microscope for the Lower Self, a telescope for the Higher Self, and a pair of reading glasses for the Middle Self. Through working with each soul we gain different vantage points from which to interpret psychic information given to us. Likewise, it also gives us different layers of reality to work with and manipulate in a magickal context. If we're just looking through one set of lenses, say reading glasses, we can't see what's going on at the microscopic level, and likewise, we cannot see what is going on at the macroscopic level beyond our eyesight like we can with a telescope. In the same vein, we work with different parts of our souls during different times and practices for specific purposes.

However, sometimes we need them to come into alignment so that we can operate from a place of being completely aligned in our divine power, working on several levels simultaneously. Most people are out of alignment with their three souls. As witches, being aligned with the three souls empowers the self to be completely plugged in with all parts of ourselves. When in a state of alignment, we're consciously aware of our multidimensional reality, being in tune with all three realms and the energies that those realms possess. It enables us to break down the barriers of the illusion of reality and to see the multidimensional reality for what it is and to see those who are in it. It increases the ability to lift the veil between the worlds and peer through.

The Trinity of the Soul

There are two pop culture metaphors I like to use to explain soul alignment. The first was suggested by Danielle Dionne, who is an amazingly talented psychic medium and witch. She compared soul alignment to the game show *Legends of the Hidden Temple* which aired on Nickelodeon in the 1990s. In the show, teams of children would compete in physical and mental competitions themed around folklore and mythology. There was one part of the challenge called "Shrine of the Silver Monkey," where essentially they came across three sections of a broken idol of a monkey deity. These sections were the head, torso, and bottom. They had to assemble the monkey idol in the right order to get it to activate and move on. First, they had to put the base on the shrine, then the torso, and then the head. This is an excellent example of soul alignment and the process—coming into alignment with the Lower Self, the Middle Self, and the Higher Self—after which you've activated your Witch Fire.

The second pop culture metaphor I like to use is even sillier. It's from *Mighty Morphin Power Rangers*, which I used to love as a child. In the show, each Power Ranger has a giant dinosaur robot that they operate. These are called Zords. In the final battle of each show, the Zords all unite to make a Megazord, which is a massive robot made from all the individual robots. I particularly like this example because each of the Zords operates autonomously but also can unite to become a much more powerful unified robot. A similar pop culture idea that parallels and predates that is the cartoon *Voltron* where the five individual robot lions come together to create a giant robot called Voltron.

The alignment of our three souls synchronizes their energy into one stream. Let's think back to the idea of binaural beats. If we think of this all in the idea of frequency, instead of two frequencies we have three. Three souls are creating something seemingly new or more precisely revealing something new from their harmonic alignment.

The Witch Fire

When our three souls are aligned a phenomenon occurs called the Witch Fire. The Witch Fire is the energetic elixir of all three of the souls functioning as one unified energy. When we align our three souls, we step into our divinity and our full potential. The Witch Fire is often experienced as an ecstatic state of gnosis, power, and Divine Love felt as agape. Agape is unconditional love for all humanity that is seen as a divine quality. It's acknowledging the divinity within all people and desiring well-being for them, often through voluntary service, whether through word, deed, or magick.

As we've explored, witches are the priests and priestesses of their own souls, and as such are their own authority on their own lives when in alignment with their True Will. The occultist Nema wrote that "the Priesthood is a condition of a soul on fire with love. The Priesthood is a way of life demanded by a certain level of spiritual responsibility, a way of life that focuses action and non-action toward universal enlightenment."[34] A famous quote from Crowley's *Book of the Law* states that "love is the Law, Love under Will."[35] Thelemites interpret this as love referring to agape and will as relating to Thelema (True Will).

The Witch Fire is also known as the Witch's Fire, Witch Flame, the Threefold Flame, and even sometimes as the Fire of the Holy Spirit. The Witch Fire is seen as electric blue and has a consistency to it that seems a bit like fire, a bit like electricity, while also moving in a fluid-like way. It permeates through the witch and around her. The Witch Fire is the power of creation itself; it's a sample of you in a deified state while being alive, the power of Spirit's Will running through you for your use in co-creating reality through magick. Here I would like to re-emphasize the nature of cocreation and not dominating or abusing this power. We seek power with, not power over. Those who have done so while working with the Witch Fire have been known to have serious repercussions. So ensure that your motives are correct and just before embracing this power. When in soul alignment and our Witch Fire is activated, it's said that we are in our divine state as a child of the Great God and the Great Goddess. The Witch Fire aligns the witch's power with the power of creation itself.

34. Nema, *The Priesthood: Parameters And Responsibilities* (Cincinnati, OH: Back Moon Publishing, 2008), 1.

35. Aleister Crowley, *The Book of the Law* (San Francisco, CA: Weiser, 1976), 9.

Exercise 60

Soul Alignment and the Witch Fire

Begin by tuning in. Pay attention to your breath as it goes in and out, bringing particular attention to the pauses between each inhalation and exhalation. Visualize your thoughts and your sense of self as the amber-colored flame of the Middle Self at your heart center, your middle cauldron. Bring your attention here as the flame grows and steadies with each breath. Keep your focus until the flame grows to fill and then encompass your body slowly.

Invoke your Lower Self and bring your attention to a point just below the navel at your lower cauldron and focus on a ruby-colored flame of the Lower Self, representing all of your primal desires, emotions, and shadows. The flame grows and steadies with each breath, slowly filling and encompassing your body, turning the amber flame to a ruby red flame.

Invoke your Higher Self and keep breathing, focus your attention on a spark of prismatic and opalescent white flame refracting all the colors of the rainbow within its whiteness just above your head. This is your Higher Self, the indestructible holy aspect of your divinity.

As you breathe, this white flame begins to pouring into the upper cauldron of your head where it begins to overflow the cauldron. The overflow of the Higher Self's energy begins pouring this white fire down through and around you like a luminous liquid fire transmuting the ruby-red flame into a flame of electric blue fire. This is your Witch Fire, the union of three parts within you that are now working together as one.

Feel the power of your Witch Fire for a few moments permeating within every cell of your body, running through your veins and gently burning around you as a divine aura. Then affirm:

"By divinity, ego, and desire
Aligned as one from three parts.
Now by the power of the Witch Fire
I am in tune with the ancient art.
Three in one and one in three
I am they and they are me."

To return back to your normal Middle Self consciousness, just perform the Closing Down exercises.

Exercise 61

Basic Hands-On Healing

The Witch Fire is the power of alignment: the power of your Higher Self, your Lower Self, and your Middle Self coming into harmony. It brings balance and helps to attune you on different levels of being, including emotional, mental, physical, and spiritual wellness. As such, we can also use it to help bring others into balance and assist in healing them. You don't need to be attuned to any lineage of energy healing, such as Reiki, for this. Through soul alignment, you're already attuned to the frequency of the ancient witch's power.

For this exercise you want to ensure that you aren't touching the person too firmly; you want your touch to be soft and gentle. The more you press, the weaker the flow of energy transference will be. You also want to ensure that you don't have any sort of technology or jewelry on your wrists or hands such as rings, bracelets, or watches. This may alter the frequency of the energy being sent by either absorbing some of the energy or by mixing its energy with the energy you're sending. For a basic method of healing, we want to rely solely on the power of our Witch Fire.

It's helpful to have the person you are doing an energy healing on to be as relaxed as you can get them, to ensure that they're more receptive to the energy and not unconsciously blocking the flow with doubts, worries, or stress. Likewise, you should already be in a relaxed and aligned state when performing this healing technique, as you should be tuned in and aligned already.

Begin by tuning in. Perform a soul alignment. Focus on the feeling of your Witch Fire all around you and running through you. Remember the energy flow from above and below you in the Creating a Circuit exercise of Tuning In (exercise 15). You want to ensure that you are never using your own personal energy reserves when healing someone else, but rather that of celestial and terrestrial energies that you're circuiting through your body and energy field. Think of the celestial and terrestrial energies as supplying fuel for your Witch Fire, to ensure you don't drain yourself in this process. Set your intentions that your Higher Self and their Higher Self, your Lower Self and their Lower Self, your Middle Self and their Middle Self are all going to work together in this process.

Awaken the energy centers in your hands (exercise 30) and gently place your hands on the person. Think about the pain, discomfort, or ailment that they're going through. Begin Solar Breathing and think of it as a bellows that is adding oxygen to your Witch Fire. Feel the energy flowing from your hands into the person you're healing. See the blue fire moving through your body and into the person's body and energy field. Focus your thoughts and feelings on the ideas of wellness, healing, and balance. Return your breath to normal while maintaining this channeled flow of energy. Tune in to the person you're healing and trust the process, knowing that your Higher Self is guiding how much energy to send and when to stop.

When you are finished have the person drink a glass of water and guide them through grounding any excess energy if they're feeling lightheaded or dizzy.

Chapter 10
BETWEEN
THE WORLDS

Before we move on to creating sacred space, I would like to explore some ideas surrounding it, the purpose being that by consciously understanding some of the theories behind it, you can consciously summon it more effectively. Sacred space is a crucial element when it comes to performing magick. In creating sacred space, we are both clearing out etheric energies and creating an etheric container for the energy raised within it. Working with etheric energy is the first step of moving energy beyond the physical level of reality. Since the etheric level is so intricately tied to the material, we can use physical and mental energy to work on this level. In other words, we can perform physical actions that have mindfulness behind them to work on the etheric.

Sacred space serves many functions. When we create sacred space, we are cleansing all physical and energetic influences that are contrary to our intentions and creating a space of protection from them. Within sacred space, we are acknowledging that there is a sacredness and inherent divinity to the area and creating a pocket within reality that transcends time and space. It is here in sacred space where we create a container within this pocket to fill with the energies that we are raising by uniting all levels of reality to merge as a singularity.

Sacred space is not just an external place. It is an internal place as well. The physical and mental serve to create, shape, and manipulate the etheric. From the etheric we can create a container for other levels of energy such as astral energy. Our internal sacred space serves as a place of stillness and emptiness wherein we can perform magick, just as the external sacred space is. It is a place of acknowledging our inherent divinity, and thereby our limitless potential of possibilities. When we are in sacred space, we are enacting a creation myth of our desire. This is the state of reality often cited in creation myths as "In the beginning…"

When we cast our sacred space, we are creating a time and space that is not a time and space through alignment. We embrace the Hermetic axiom of "As above, so below," meaning we recognize and acknowledge that events that occur on the macrocosm affect events that occur on the microcosm. Macrocosm means the larger Universe and microcosm means the smaller Universe. For example, outer space is the macrocosm, and our world is a microcosm. Our world is a macrocosm to the microcosm of our bodies. Our bodies are the macrocosm to the microcosm of our cells and DNA. All levels of reality are linked, and the cause on one level affects the other level.

The Butterfly Effect

This ties into the idea of the butterfly effect, a term coined by Edward Lorenz, a mathematician and pioneer of chaos theory. The idea behind the butterfly effect is that small causes can amount to more substantial results. The illustration given for the metaphor is the tiniest butterfly flapping its wings in one part of the world. That flapping moves the wind, and that movement of the wind eventually leads to a tornado in another part of the world through an endless series of causes and effects. In this notion, a small change on the minute level creates a drastic change on the broader scale.

Likewise, what we do internally affects the world around us and the world around us affects our inner world. With this notion, nothing is separate, and our inner and outer world are intricately tied to one another. This embraces the next part of the axiom "As above, so below," which is "As within, so without." In *The Kybalion*, which popularized these Hermetic concepts and axioms, it states that the nature of the physical Universe is composed of thoughts emanating from the All, or the Universal Mind of Source. This notion suggests that we as humans, having the ability to think, conjure, hold, and control ideas, are thereby able also to influence and create reality, which is what we call magick.

We know that when we zoom out, looking at the images of outer space from satellites, that the Universe tends to move in spirals and orbital systems, such as solar systems. We also know that when we zoom in deeply with powerful microscopes that atoms move in orbital systems, such as electrons circling a nucleus. As above, so below. This implies that the Universe is fractal. A fractal is when a larger image can be broken into smaller pieces and still contain the blueprint and model of the whole within it. A single cell contains within it all of the information of what the cell is a part of, within its DNA.

Holographic Reality

When we tie in the idea that the Universe is mental, and thoughts within the Universal Mind, we get the notion that the Universe is holographic. A hologram is also fractal, with each part containing the larger image. Fractal cosmology seems to be in alignment with this idea. Fractal cosmology is a theory by physicists that the Universe is inherently fractal, and sometimes believed to be self-generating through this fractal nature. The central concept to remember is that every particle of matter contains the blueprint of the entire Universe from the Big Bang. This strongly implies that the information of the whole Universe is within us.

What is different about holograms, in a nutshell, is that the three-dimensional illusion of a hologram is formed from light and the image that is being projected is nonlocal. Our brains work similarly. All the images we see and sounds we hear and other sensory information initially originates from somewhere outside of our heads. However, the brain takes this external information and processes it, allowing us to perceive the world. The mind can be tricked as well, perceiving things that aren't there as if they are there. This is demonstrated with hallucinations as well as hypnotic suggestions, and this indicates that reality is more subjectively perception-based than objectively concrete and real.

Many philosophers and theologians have grappled with the question of whether reality is a dream, and whether we are the dreamer or the dreamed. In Hermetic philosophy, the answer is both. We are but the dreams and thoughts of the Infinite Mind, but as microcosms of the Infinite Mind, we are also dreamers. If we can focus our attention on both the microcosmic inner space of mind and the macrocosmic outer space of physical reality, we can create profound levels of sacred space.

The Magick Circle

The most common form of sacred space to the witch is the magick circle. The circle is a symbol of the infinite and finite. It is everything and nothing. It is the Ouroboros, the serpent eating its own tail, symbolic of the never-ending cycle of creation and destruction, birth and death, and a symbol of the cosmos without beginning or end.

There are four primary purposes for the magick circle: protection, containment, liminality, and paradox. While most witches cast a magick circle, it's important to note that not all do. Some witches will cast a circle for every working they do, some will only do so when they feel it's appropriate. While this is a personal choice of discernment, I feel anyone starting out with working with magick is served well by always casting a magick circle.

The magick circle is created to put a barrier between yourself and everything else in your environment. The idea is that it is sort of like casting a force field where no energies or entities may enter without your explicit invitation. Some practitioners of magick see the magick circle as an extension of their own aura, and the act of expanding it is so only that which you allow in your own personal field of energy is permitted and everything else must keep out.

As a container for energy, the magick circle serves to store all the energy that you're raising and calling into the sacred space, where it can then blend and weld together through your will and intention to birth the spell itself. The metaphor I like the best for this is the idea of a cauldron: you're adding different ingredients, and within the cauldron they all meld together to create something entirely different. You can also think of this as the modern-day equivalent of the Crockpot. You add in the right amount of different ingredients and allow it to cook and come together to create a specific food that didn't exist before every item was added and heated up together.

"Betwixt and between" is a traditional witchcraft phrase for the state of liminality, in which the witch operates. The magick circle serves as the creation of liminal space. The liminal is the threshold of being neither here nor there, neither now nor then. For the witch, the liminal is a state of being of pure potential. It's the nexus point where raw energy converges. This is why certain places are considered powerful in regard to witchcraft, such as the crossroads where two paths merge but aren't quite either, or the shore where the ocean bleeds into the land. Times such as midnight are liminal in nature; midnight has been referred to as the "witching hour" and is seen as a powerful time to create magick. In liminal spaces, you don't have to decide to be in this world or the otherworld. You're simultaneously in both without being in either.

I often think of the cast magick circle as the "Wood Between the Worlds" in C. S. Lewis's *The Magician's Nephew*, the first story in the Chronicles of Narnia. When I was a very young child, this was one of my favorite book series, and while there are very strong Christian themes within the stories, there's also a lot of magick and Pagan influences within the story as well. In the story, the Wood Between the Worlds is a place of stillness and timelessness. It isn't itself a world, yet it is in its own right. The Wood Between the Worlds is not only a place that isn't a place, but it's also a time of timelessness. In it, time doesn't exist. There's just an eternal moment now, while ages may pass in the worlds outside of it. I have always found it interesting and amusing that to get to this place, the characters use magick rings, which are circles.

There's a paradoxical nature of the magick circle. A paradox is a concept that has a self-contradictory nature, yet holds greater significance when meditated upon than its surface appearance. Like the Ouroboros, a circle is also our symbol of nothingness, the number zero. Zero is simultaneously nothing and something. Zero is infinite yet finite in its nature. When we create sacred space we are sanctifying the space, meaning we are setting it aside to be made holy or sacred. In witchcraft, there is nothing that is not sacred in existence, yet we are still sanctifying the space by setting it aside as holy space, something that would seem paradoxical if everything is already holy.

Within the magick circle, symbolic of infinity, there is a sectioned off space being contained. Within the circle, we are acknowledging the infinite reality of which we are a part of and cannot separate ourselves from. When we are casting a circle, we are partitioning ourselves and our space, separating it from time and place, and creating a container for energy. We are laying down firm boundaries by recreating boundlessness. We are protecting ourselves and our magickal operations by surrounding ourselves with endlessness.

Paradox is at the heart of the mysteries of witchcraft. I believe that paradox is what allows the conditions for the witch to create magick. By creating a paradox, we essentially overload the processing of reality by breaking the rules. In a way, we're jamming the system like throwing a wrench into the cogs, where we can then enter in our own codes for when we're done and the system and its processes of reality resume. When casting a circle a phrase that is often used is "a space beyond space" and "a time beyond time." What this is implying is that it is a space that is not a space and contains a time that is not a time. By creating such a thing we are essentially hacking the nature of reality through circle casting.

When we are creating sacred space through circle casting, we are centering our energy on a deeper level. The main difference between centering yourself, as mentioned earlier, and casting the circle, is that you are not just focusing your internal awareness and energy, but you are now creating an energetic matrix of expanded consciousness to operate within. You see, the circle isn't just a two-dimensional circle, but rather a three-dimensional sphere, a bubble of reality, similar to the aura.

Figure 8: Ouroboros

Exercise 62

Painting with Light

To paint the air with light is an important component of circle casting that will take it from being a noir experience into being a clairvoyant experience. It's also an important aspect of using the invoking and banishing pentagrams, which we will get to later. Once you've mastered the ability to paint with light in the air, you can use it for other situations as well, as it's not limited to these uses. You can use it to mark your personal energetic space, by writing your name in the four directions of the place that you are. You can also use it to draw sigils and glyphs of power within the air to channel its influence.

Tune in. Begin to use Elemental Breathing but we're going to add a few more steps. Once you have a rhythm, start drawing energy up through you from your feet to your crown upon inhalation. While pausing your breath before exhalation, see energy spiraling up around your body. On exhalation draw energy down from your crown and through you to your feet. While pausing your breath before inhalation, see energy spiraling down around your body. Mentally chant "earth, air, fire, water" as normal and when you feel enough energy has been built up, breathe as normal.

Perform the Shielding exercise. When you're done, use the pointer finger of your projective hand, the hand you write with and intend to direct the energy you've built up through your finger. Use your visualization skills with your eyes open, and with strong intention draw a foot-sized "O" of light in front of you, made of an electric-blue and white light. This would be similar to if you had a glowstick in the dark and moved it quickly, leaving a trail of colored light. However, you want to maintain focus and keep visualizing the light streak remaining.

Move your other (receptive) hand as if it were a vacuum over the "O" of light that you drew in front of you, sucking it back into your energy field, still keeping your eyes open. Alternate this exercise by doing it with your eyes closed and then your eyes open. When you feel you've truly mastered this, you can move on to casting the circle.

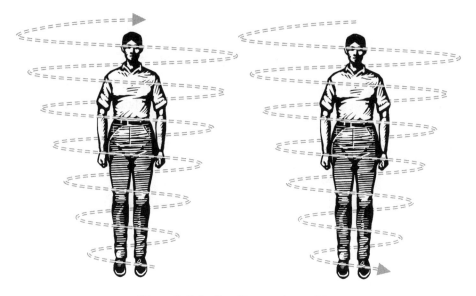

Figure 9: Spiraling Energy Around You

Exercise 63

Casting and Releasing the Circle

Tune in. Perform a soul alignment. Stand to face the north. With your projective arm stretched out, point your finger outward. Just like the previous exercise, begin to paint the air with the blue Witch Fire. While you walk or turn around, depending on your space, say out loud:

> *"I cast this circle to create a space beyond space and a time beyond time."*

Keep drawing in the air with your finger to create a ring around yourself of this blue energy until eventually reaching the north again. Continue another round, stating:

> *"I cast this circle to block out any energies and spirits that are not allies of mine."*

When reaching north again, perform one last pass around, and state:

> *"I cast this circle so that all energies raised herein will be confined."*

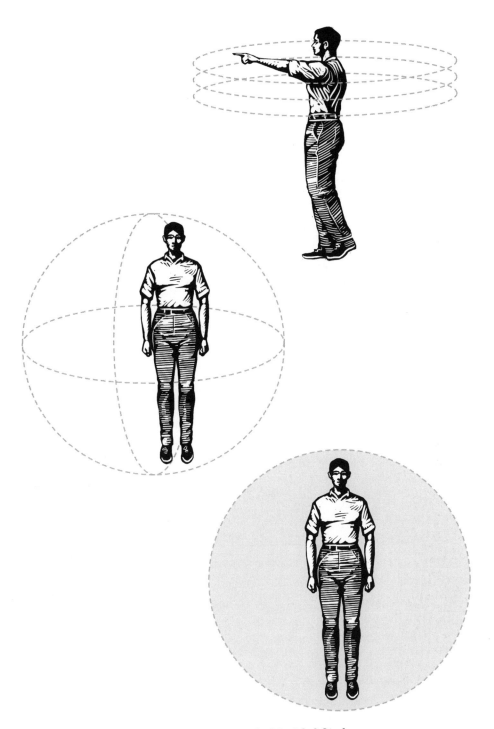

Figure 10: Casting the Magickal Circle

Facing north, raise your hand palm up to the sky. As you do so, see the ring of the circle expanding to form a dome above you. State:

"As above!"

Turn your palm facedown and begin lowering it, pushing down the ring of the circle to expand to form a dome below you. State:

"So below! The circle is sealed!"

Stomp your foot firmly into the ground or clap your hands, asserting your willpower of your circle casting.

After performing your magick, you will want to release the circle. To release the circle, take your receptive hand and extend it outward, moving counterclockwise starting at the north and pushing the ring of light away with your hand as if you were opening a heavy curtain surrounding you, simultaneously envisioning it entering the palm of your hand. The circle is now open. Feel all the energy of your magick rushing out into the Universe to begin manifesting.

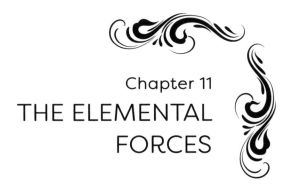

Chapter 11

THE ELEMENTAL FORCES

W e enhance sacred space for the purposes of magick by bringing in the energies of the elemental forces to assist us in creating an area that is beyond time and space. The elemental powers are the energetic building blocks of creation, so the witch summons those elemental forces through portals within the sacred space. If we think of sacred space as a container of energy, the elemental portals are what hold and empower this space and bring in that raw energy that the Universe is composed of.

However, the elemental energy coming through those portals may be too intense or too mild for the space we are trying to create. The witch bypasses this by calling upon a guardian of each elemental force. The guardian of each element is considered a master of that type of energy, and as such is called upon to control the flow of elemental energy entering so that it is sufficient for the working that we are doing. The elemental guardian also serves as a guardian of that portal to ensure nothing but raw elemental energy enters the space.

One of the first concepts one usually encounters within witchcraft is the concept of the four elements along with the fifth. I often find that books that discuss the true heart of the four elements don't do a thorough job for the beginner. The four elements are earth, air, fire, and water, and the fifth element is spirit. These elements were defined by ancient Greek philosophers and alchemists by that name, though similar ideas were also used in ancient Indian and Egyptian theology. Later, medieval alchemists expanded upon these four elements by subdividing them into further elements, such as Suflur, Mercury, Lead, Phosophorus, etc. Alchemy was the forbearer of chemistry and as such gave birth to the elemental periodic table.

What is important to understand about these elements is that their names are symbolic and metaphorical. They are not literally earth, air, fire, or water—nor are they the spirit that rules these things. Instead, they are names for the different types of energy. The periodic table took the further defined and articulated metaphors of the four elements and looked at the purely chemical composition of these ideas. The metaphorical became literal. This has caused a lot of confusion surrounding the concept of elements in modern times. Because it can be confusing when talking about the elemental force versus its physical symbol, I will capitalize the first letter of an elemental force when talking about it.

Elemental Building Blocks

The word element denotes the building blocks which compose all things and exist within all things inside this Universe. Therefore, if you were to pick up a clump of soil, it is not purely earth. Instead, the soil contains all four of the elements within it. The same is true for water, wind, and fire. These qualities of energy that compose all things were described by ancients with these four names because the energy acts and moves in a very similar manner energetically to their physical counterpart.

As I mentioned earlier, we as humans do not have an exact way to describe energy as we perceive it, as our vocabulary for it is very underdeveloped for such things. With the Hermetic idea of "As above, so below," we can get an idea of how the unseen forces work by observing the forces we can experience with our five senses. So by pointing at the metaphorical counterpart of the element, we can begin to understand its nature and quality a bit easier and describe and discuss it with other people and have them know what we're talking about.

Understanding that the elemental names are symbolic is hard to grasp unless one can psychically experience them. For example, Water is a relatively lighter and colder energy that is very wet and fluid-feeling in nature and tends to have a flowing quality to it. It is usually perceived as being a cool temperature. Therefore, water is an excellent metaphor for the element of Water. The element of Earth has a very slow and stable energy to it; is perceived as cool temperature-wise; is dry; and is very dense. The element of Fire, on the other hand, is lighter energy of constant fluctuation, instability, and rapid shifting. It is perceived as having a very hot temperature to it; it is dry, and usually has a bit of a tingling sensation about it. The element of Air is a quicker energy that is perceived as warmer, wet, and has a flowing energy to it, similar to a gust of a steady wind.

We could easily call Water "cold and wet energy," Earth could be called "cool and dry energy," Fire can be named "hot and dry energy," and Air could be called "hot and wet energy." However, this is a mouthful and also doesn't fully denote what the energy's essential, inherent nature is, but rather how it acts and feels when experienced. The problem also arises that the "coolness" of Water and the "coolness" of Earth are also different experiences. This is also true with the stability of Air and the stability of Earth, two very different sensations. This is why elements are so much easier to use as descriptors for these energies. Also, by having a metaphor for these types of energy we have a much easier way of discerning, interacting, and summoning them. By working with symbolism, we are consciously working with the subconscious and the universal language of the Collective Unconscious.

Quintessence

Spirit, the fifth element, is a bit of a paradox in itself and is also fractal. Spirit is the finest element which composes all of the four elements but also contains within it all four elements. Each element contains Spirit, and each of the four elements are held within Spirit and in a state of perfected balance. This is the quintessence of the elements. It is the quintessential raw energy that binds all things together and the thing that includes all things, yet the thing which all things are composed of. For this reason, Spirit, just like the magick circle or the Ouroboros, is often symbolized by the paradoxical circle.

The elements also have qualities to them that correspond to states of physical existence. Water has an emotional quality to it. Earth has a growing quality to it and, as the slowest vibration element, is the most solid or tangible. Air has a mental and intellectual condition to it and Fire has an animating quality to it, most often likened to that inner divine spark. The elemental system gives us the best way to begin categorizing energy and, as the energy composes all things, it is the building blocks of reality. Therefore, if we are reenacting a creation myth within our magick circle, the next thing that we are going to want to do is have a palette of these magickal building blocks of energy to work with.

Since the elements represent the most basic energetic components of reality, it also tends to be a popular categorization system for various concepts, virtues, challenges, and attributes. It tends to be one of the primary systems of correspondences that witches use. Correspondence, in its most basic definition, is when something has a distinctly strong energetic resonance with a specific archetypal energy signature such as an element or a planet. We will explore both correspondences and planets in more detail shortly, but for now, it's sufficient to explain that certain things seem to have a stronger energetic resonance with one element than others despite containing all of the elemental building blocks of energy within them. This is not just limited to physical things or physical forces but also to more abstract concepts, states of being, and experiences. Each element also corresponds to one of the three worlds. As we explore or talk about elements, try to think less literally and more symbolically. This will help you to unlock the mysteries of the elemental forces.

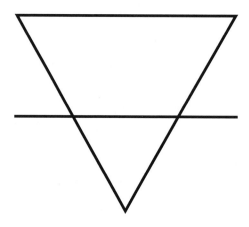

Figure 11: Earth Glyph

Earth

The element of Earth is that of form, stability, stillness, and growth. It is closely tied to physical things, being the slowest and densest of the four elemental energies. Just like the namesake of this element, the qualities of Earth as a whole are that of rootedness, stability, abundance, strength, growth, structure, birth, and detail. It is an energy of structure, formation, geometry, and crystallization.

Earth is the element tied to the mysteries of "tomb and womb," that of creation and return. This is understood through its symbol of soil. Plants grow and feast upon the soil, taking up nutrients. Animals, people, and insects eat those plants. However, all things placed within the ground of the earth will eventually be consumed through decomposition and return to it, including us, until the cycle starts again. We know the element of Earth within us as our physical bodies and physical health. We connect with Earth through growth, exercise, physical and financial security, structure, organization, and groundedness. Earth provides the ability for things to be experienced as physical. Earth is related to the sense of touch and the psychic experience of clairtangency (clear feeling).

As a state of matter, it is represented by the solid state, with slowly vibrating molecules creating a crystallization of form. It is almost universally associated with the direction of the north. The types of intelligence connected with Earth are called gnomes, which are envisioned as short and stout humanoid figures that are associated with both gardening and growing plants as well as digging and mining precious minerals and gemstones from within the earth. The glyph of Earth is a downward triangle indicating it's passive energy with a negative charge, and a line running through it to denote that it's a generative force.

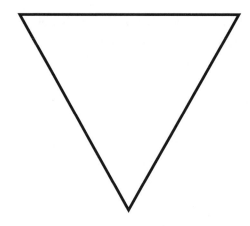

Figure 12: Water Glyph

Water

The element of Water is that of expression, responsiveness, synthesis, and magnetism. It is closely tied to things of an emotional and intuitive nature. Water expresses itself in many ways and many forms, from the still pond, to the gently moving stream, to the raging tidal waves crashing against each other. It takes on the shape of whatever container that it is placed in and it synthesizes and mixes with any additional water or liquid that it comes across. It can be as subtle as a mist or as intense as a waterfall.

We know the element of Water within us as our emotional, dreaming, and intuitive nature. We connect with Water through dreaming, honoring our emotions, adaptability, psychic visions, astral projection, nurturing relationships, and self-care. We experience Water as nourishment, healing, flow, empathy, sensitivity, intensity, mysticism, and depth. Water moves in cycles, like the ebb and flow of tides, or the moon which moves those tides and has its own cycle of waxing and waning. Water is related to the sense of taste and the psychic experience of clairgustance (clear taste) as well as clairempathy (clear emotion), both of which are acts of taking energy in and absorbing it.

As a state of matter, it is represented by the liquid state, whose molecules are vibrating at a steady state making it too slow to be gas and too fast to be solid. It is almost universally associated with the direction of the west. The forms of intelligence connected with Water are called undines, which are portrayed as little merfolk composed of water. The glyph of Water is a downward triangle indicating it's passive energy with a negative charge. There's no line running through it as with the glyph for Earth, because it is a generated force, just as water bubbles up from underground wells or emerges through the liquefaction of a solid.

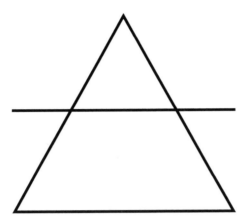

Figure 13: Air Glyph

Air

The element of Air is that of space and movement. We know the element of Air the best not by seeing it, but rather experiencing what it's distributing. We know Air by the scents that travel through the breezes, and the sounds being transported through it; we feel the temperatures that the wind moves and carries; we see the leaves and dust that spin and dance around within its whirlwinds.

We know the element of Air within us as our mental and intellectual nature. Air is the expanse of stillness from which intelligence, intellect, analysis, communication, sound, creativity, awareness, and movement emerge and move. We connect with Air through intellectual endeavors, meditation, visualization, concentration, imagination, speaking, singing, and listening. Air is related to the sense of smell and hearing and the psychic experiences of clairalience (clear smelling) and clairaudience (clear hearing).

The natural symbolic representations of Air are wind, breezes, tornadoes, smoke, and thunder. As a state of matter, it is expressed as gas, which is also formless, light, and warm. It is most commonly associated with the direction of the east. The forms of intelligence connected with Air are called sylphs, which are portrayed as wispy sprite-like creatures. The glyph of Air is an upward triangle indicating it's active energy with a positive charge and a line running through it to denote that it's a generative force.

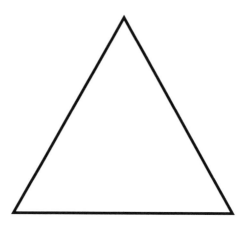

Figure 14: Fire Glyph

Fire

The element of Fire is closely tied to things of a passionate and transformative nature. It is a kinetic force that exists through movement and action. If it were to stop moving it would lose its power, just like a wildfire—and just like a wildfire, it seems to have a determined, aggressive willpower of its own. Fire is transformational, an energy that transmutes anything that comes across it, just as fire turns to char and ash anything it comes across.

The qualities of Fire as a whole are that of passion, drive, willpower, transformation, warmth, and power. We know Fire as our own spirit. We connect with Fire within ourselves through sexuality, ambition, intensity, determination, and courage. It is the spark of potential that creates a fully animated fire. It is the power of magma erupting and overcoming anything that comes across it. It is the seemingly eternal light and glow from the sun and of the stars, imposing their own will upon our planet and our life. Fire is related to the sense of vision and the psychic experience of clairvoyance (clear vision).

As a state of matter, it is expressed as plasma, which is unstable, ever-shifting, lightweight, and dangerous, just like its earthly symbol of fire. Lightning is plasma, as are stars. Plasma occurs when gas has absorbed so much energy that the electrons become separated from their nuclei. These electrons become ionized and electrical, creating light and electromagnetic radiation. In fact, in some cases if a fire is hot enough the gases it emits will become plasma.

It is most commonly associated with the direction of the south. The forms of intelligence connected with Fire are called salamanders, which are portrayed as small lizards composed of fire. The glyph of Fire is an upward triangle indicating it's active energy with a positive charge. There's no line running through it as with the glyph for Air because it is a generated force. Fire is sustained with Air just as plasma is generated from gas.

Figure 15: The Pentagram and the Elements

The Pentagram

There are no other symbols more closely tied to witchcraft than the pentagram and pentacle. The word *pentagram* comes from the Greek word *pentagrammon* meaning "five-lined." Thus, pentagrams are five-pointed geometric stars, and pentacles are pentagrams with a circle around them. Neither symbol is a sign of evil or devil-worship whether it is right side up or upside down. The pentagram has a history that is hard to pinpoint, but we find it in almost every religious and mystical tradition, including those of the Greek, Babylonian, Celtic, Egyptian, Druid, Kabbalistic, Christian, and Chinese.

Witches view pentagrams as a symbol of balance, protection, and divinity. The pentagram represents the four elements with the top point being the fifth element of quintessence or divinity. An upright pentagram represents the material ascending to the spiritual, while a reversed pentagram represents spirit descending into matter. If a pentagram is upright, going clockwise from the top point of quintessence Spirit, we have the element of Water in the upper right-hand point, Fire in the lower right-hand point, Earth in the lower left-hand point, and Air in the upper left-hand point.

Witches and ceremonial magicians often use pentagrams drawn in the air with directed energy as keys to open and close elemental portals of energy. When the pentagram is being used to open a portal of elemental energy, it's called an "invoking pentagram," and when it's being used to close down a portal of elemental energy, it's called a "banishing pentagram."

The invoking and banishing pentagrams come from the ceremonial traditions to bring an elemental force into the circle or working. In the witchcraft traditions we wouldn't call this invoking; rather we would call this evoking, because we are not calling this energy into our body but rather into our magick circle. In witchcraft, the word invoking is usually in reference to calling something into your body or into an object, whereas the word evoking is used to call something into your space. But in the ceremonial traditions they view the circle as an extension of their body, so when they're calling something into the circle, they're invoking it. Likewise, since some witches see the magickal circle as an extension of their aura, it could definitely be seen as invoking. The invoking and banishing pentagrams can be seen as "keys," but I see them more as portals. The invoking pentagrams open up a portal for a specific elemental energy to come through, and the banishing pentagrams close a portal's flow of a specific elemental energy.

In ritual, these pentagrams are drawn when calling upon elemental guardians who will be in charge of the portals and controlling via their discernment how much energy to allow through that portal, based on their expertise of that element and the working itself. These pentagrams can also be used without calling upon a guardian if you aren't performing a ritual to control the elemental energies of a place or object.

Before invoking a pentagram, it's essential to connect with each element first on a deep level and understand how that energy feels. Once you're appropriately attuned to that element you can then summon that feeling from within you and channel it by focusing on it while painting the energy into the air. You paint the energy in the air in the same manner as you would casting a circle, but with the focus of the elemental energy.

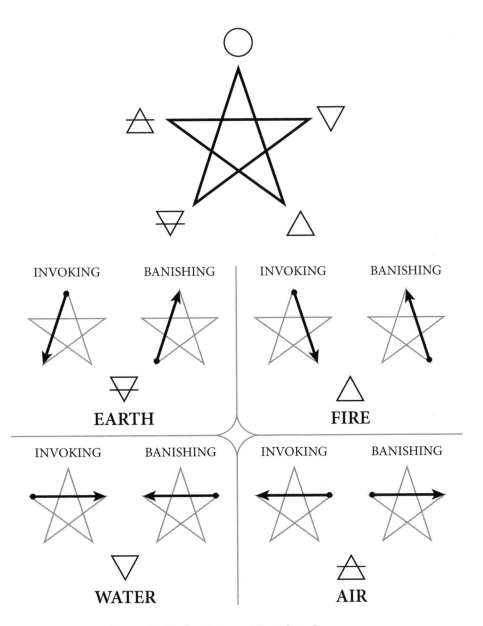

Figure 16: The Invoking and Banishing Pentagrams

Exercise 64

Attuning to the Elements

Begin by tuning in. Take a deep breath and state:

"I intend to vibrate in resonance with the element
of Earth, so that I may know you."

In the air before you, draw the invoking pentagram of Earth in blue Witch Fire. Feel the energy of Earth emanating from your pentagram portal. Feel the energy of the element of Earth surround you. Perform the Elemental Breathing exercise, except focus only on Earth with each count, repeating Earth to four counts of every part of the breathing process. Take in the energy of Earth, let it charge and fill you. Bring your breath and awareness to fill each cauldron one by one with this energy. Fill it in the lower cauldron, the middle cauldron, and the upper cauldron. What does it feel like? What does it look like? What does it smell like? What does it sound like? What does it taste like? When you are done, perform the banishing pentagram of the Earth.

Continue this with the other elements (Air, Fire, Water, and Spirit) with their appropriate invoking pentagrams and banishing pentagrams.

Exercise 65

Conjuring Elemental Energy for Charging and Sending

Begin by tuning in. Activate your palm energy centers. Decide which element you want to conjure. Draw the invoking pentagram of that element with the fingers of your projective hand on the palm of your receptive hand. Begin focusing on what the specific element feels like, based on your experiences from the previous exercise. Hold your hands apart. Fill each of your internal cauldrons with the elemental energy and then visualize them streaming out into each hand, creating an orb of energy formed purely of that element. Visualize the elemental symbol on your orb.

You can use this energy to charge objects with a specific element. For example, if I wanted to charge a candle with the element of Air, I would take the Air elemental energy in my hands and place it around the candle, visualizing all of that elemental energy filling and activating the candle. You can also send this orb of energy to another person over distance. Solely focus on the energy orb inside of your hands, think of the recipient, and take a deep breath. Exhale forcefully, visualizing that you are blowing the sphere of elemental energy to its destination.

Exercise 66

Calling the Quarters

The quarters are the four directional spots within a circle where the guardian spirits of the four elements preside.

Begin by tuning in and performing a soul alignment. Starting in the north draw the invoking pentagram of its corresponding element before you in blue Witch Fire light. Call forth the guardian of that element while visualizing the guardian coming forward, and raising your receptive hand. Start at the north and move clockwise in your circle:

"Hail to the Guardian of the Watchtower of the [Direction],
By the power of [Element] and Astral Light,
I [your name] summon, stir, and call you forth in this circle,
To witness, guard, and join in this rite,
Ancient One come and take your place,
Bring forth your power and open your gates,
Stationing your quarter in this sacred space.
Hail and welcome!"

Wait until you feel their presence. Then, starting from the center of your pentagram trace a line in blue Witch Fire light to your next quarter point moving from north/Earth to east/Air to south/Fire to west/Water and finishing by connecting your trail of light from the western pentacle to the northern pentacle.

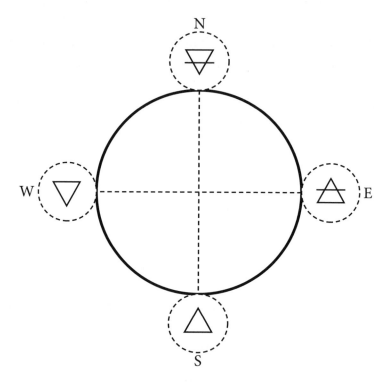

Figure 17: Invoking Watchtower in the Elemental Quarters

Exercise 67

Dismissing the Quarters

This process is similar to Calling the Quarters but done in reverse. To dismiss the quarters, you move counterclockwise from the west to the north, draw the banishing pentagram of the appropriate element before you in blue Witch Fire light. Call to the guardian of the element while visualizing the guardian leaving the space, while raising your projective hand:

"Hail to the Guardian of the Watchtower of the [Direction],
By the power of [Element] and Astral Light,
I thank you for your presence and assistance,
In guarding, and protecting this rite,
Stay if you will and leave if you must,
May there always be peace between us,
In perfect love and in perfect trust.
Hail and farewell!"

Walk counterclockwise repeating this process to dismiss each quarter with its guardian.

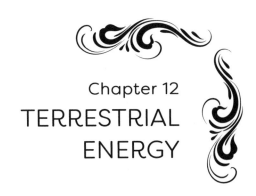

Chapter 12
TERRESTRIAL
ENERGY

Witches tend to be animists. The word "animist" refers to one who embraces the concept of animism. Animism is derived from the words *anima* and *animus*, the Latin words relating to the soul, intelligence, and having a living nature. In the eyes of the witch, everything is alive, and anything with physical matter contains life force and intelligence. For the witch, nature is alive. The rocks, the water, the wind, the animals, the plants, the stars, the planets, and all things that we can perceive as existing within the material Universe.

As all things come from and are imbued with the quintessence of Spirit, all things are holy and alive in their own right—and anything that has a physical existence contains within it a unique personality, energy, and expression of Spirit. In Sacred Fires, we call this Universal Spirit the Star Goddess, the spirit of the Universe itself, and will often use the terms Star Goddess and Universe interchangeably. The Star Goddess as a primary aspect of Spirit pervades everything that exists perceivably and unperceivably within the Universe.

Before we begin looking outward to the energies of different planets and stars, let's start with our own planet that we're living upon. Just as humans have individual expressions of identity yet are plugged into a Collective Unconscious of humanity that connects them as a species on a spiritual level, so too is nature. A plant carries the collective memory of its species, and each plant has its own individual spirit. The same is true for crystals, animals, and other expressions of nature.

Just as humans can access the Collective Unconscious and its wisdom and history, as well as the ancestral river of blood, so too do other forms of life. For example, an owl is an individual animal with its consciousness, but it's also plugged in to the broader Collective Consciousness of all owls. A rosebush has its own individual personality and yet it is part of the larger memory and spirit of roses. Each piece of amethyst has its own identity and is also part of the larger amethyst memory.

The Earth Is Alive

Witches understand that the planet itself is alive. The idea that the earth is alive isn't just a spiritual concept. Chemist James Lovelock and microbiologist Lynn Margulis proposed the idea that the earth is alive and called this the Gaia Theory.[36] To avoid confusion with the element of Earth, I will refer to planet earth as a being as Gaia, derived from the name Gaea, the ancient Greek name for the spirit of our planet. The main idea behind the Gaia Theory is that our planet earth acts as a single intelligent self-regulating system, much like an organism, and in turn, all life on planet earth is just part of a more extensive network. This is something that witches have always known; Gaia is alive and we as humans, as well as the rest of nature, are just microcosmic parts that are co-dependent with the planet. This is similar to how we as humans have tons of micro-organisms and bacteria within us that allows us to live, digest, and heal ourselves. As such, witches are often reverent to Gaia and see themselves as having a divine mission to be caretakers, protectors, and stewards of our planet.

Raven Grimassi discusses a fascinating concept that he terms "The Organic Memory of the Earth," in which all things decompose and become part of the land itself.[37] As I previously discussed, our blood contains the genetic memories of our ancestors. The experience, memories, wisdom, and history of all biological matter are absorbed back into Gaia when we die and decompose within her or our ashes are scattered. Gaia holds all of this wisdom within her.

36. James Locklove, *Gaia, a New Look at Life on Earth* (Oxford, NY: Oxford University Press, 1995).
37. Raven Grimassi, *Grimoire of the Thorn-Blooded Witch: Mastering the Five Arts of Old World Witchery* (San Francisco, CA: Weiser, 2014) xvii–xix.

Grimassi likens this to the Akashic Records of Eastern thought, but being independent of it and residing within Gaia.

Witches, shamans, and mystics have known for a long time that crystals are not only alive with specific energies but that they also record memory. In fact, we use crystals to operate most of our computer technology due to their ability to receive, hold, and project information. When we zoom in on dirt with powerful microscopes, what do we see? We see that it's made up of tiny organisms, decomposing plant and animal matter, minerals, and crystals. These crystals are recording all the information of what is being devoured by Gaia, and the land contains the memories of all that have existed upon it, from dinosaurs to our ancestors.

Syncing to the Earth's Imagination

But does Gaia have a consciousness? The surface of the planet earth and the ionosphere work together to create electromagnetic rhythmic pulses produced by lightning activity within a cavity. Our world gives off an electromagnetic pulse of 7.83 hertz cycles (though it can spike at times) and has been compared by many researchers to the brain activity of humans and all other animals with a brain. This mysterious electromagnetic pulsing cycle is referred to as the Schumann Resonance, named after physicist Winfried Otto Schumann, who was the first to predict this phenomenon mathematically.[38]

Independently, nuclear physicist Robert Beck examined the brainwave states of witches, psychics, Christian faith healers, shamans, and other healers, and discovered that the majority of them exhibit the brainwave pattern of 7.8–8 hertz cycles when healing or getting into an altered state of consciousness.[39]

We've already explored this brainwave state earlier; this is the alpha brainwave state (7.5–13 hertz) linked with psychic ability, meditation, daydreaming, and visualization. So if the Schumann Resonance is the mind of Gaia, this would lead one to conclude that the consciousness of Gaia is in alpha, and perhaps when we slip into alpha we are aligning ourselves to

---

38. James L. Oschman, *Energy Medicine: The Scientific Basis* (Dover, NH: Elsevier, 2016), 257–263.

39. Barbara Brennan, *Light Emerging: The Journey of Personal Healing* (Broadway, NY: Bantam, 1993), 17–18.

the consciousness, dreams, imagination, and memories of Gaia herself. This dream-altered state of consciousness is associated with the astral. As such, we are influenced by Gaia and Gaia is affected by us.

Exercise 68

❦

Connecting to Gaia

Find somewhere in nature where you will be undisturbed. Begin by tuning in and invoking your Lower Self—as the Lower Self is the part of us that is connected with the earth. Sit in a comfortable position upon the ground and place your hands upon the earth. From a place deep within your heart and spirit call out to Gaia, seeing this call as an energetic impulse of waves moving through your body and down through your hands, reaching down to the heart of Gaia. Verbally or mentally affirm:

> *"Hand to land*
> *Bone to stone*
> *Blood to mud*
> *To Gaia's mind*
> *I am aligned.*
> *I am aligned*
> *To Gaia's mind*
> *Mud to blood*
> *Stone to bone*
> *Land to hand."*

Wait for a response from Gaia. This will be different for every individual. Pay attention to all your inner clair-senses. I usually first begin receiving this as a clairtangent feeling before an image of her appears in my Witch Eye. When you get a response, feel free to start a conversation with Gaia, asking her questions, advice, or if there's a message that she has for you. I recommend building a relationship with Gaia for many reasons, chief among them is that she is the queen and mother of the earthly realm. In this role, she can assist with work involving the Spirit of Place or nature spirits when the need arises, if you connect with her in this manner and ask for her assistance.

When you are done, you may simply close down to return to Middle Self consciousness.

The Spirit of Place

While Gaia has a consciousness of her own, different locations, as well as buildings themselves also have their own forms of consciousness. This is usually referred to as the Spirit of Place. Within the Spirit of Place there may also be plants, animals, minerals, and other spirits that inhabit it, and have their own individual forms of consciousness—just as there are physical ecosystems of plants and animals co-existing and creating complex systems of community. A psychic witch should learn to connect with not only Gaia herself but also the Spirits of Place and the spirits within places.

Making friends with the Spirit of Place is important. By befriending the Spirit of Place any magickal endeavors that you perform in that location— be it a forest, a beach, a house, or a garden—will have the blessing of the Spirit of Place, ensuring greater results in your magick and providing protection and less resistance from spirits that may be dwelling there. Think about it. You wouldn't want some stranger barging into your home and performing strange rituals, would you? Probably not.

When engaging a Spirit of Place there are a few important factors to keep in mind. You always want to ask for permission. Heed and respect the answer, especially if it's a no. You always want to make an offering if you are a visitor. Offerings are going to vary based upon where you live and the customs of that place. Try to research different religious, indigenous, shamanic, and folklore customs when it comes to land offerings—that will give you a strong idea of what the land likes.

Here in New England where I live, it's customary to offer cornmeal, tobacco, fresh water, or a strand of your hair—especially if you are foraging or harvesting things from that location. Never take from nature without giving something back. There's an old saying that "a gift demands a gift." This keeps equal exchange and reverence for nature so that you aren't just taking and taking and upsetting the Spirit of Place. As you grow a bond with the Spirit of Place, you can ask it what sort of offerings it enjoys.

Exercise 69

Connecting to the Spirit of Place

At the threshold of the location you are looking to connect with, such as the edge of a forest or outside the door of a house, begin tuning in and invoking your Lower Self. Perform the last exercise (Connecting to Gaia), calling to Gaia and connecting with her with your hands on the ground of the barrier of whatever location you're at.

Provide an offering while calling out either verbally or mentally. It can go something like this:

> *"I call to the Spirit of this Place, I [name] bring you an offering of [offering] to honor and connect with you. I ask for your permission and blessing to [explain what your purpose is for connecting to the place. Are you wanting to perform magick, meditate, or something else? Let the Spirit of Place know]. Do I have your permission and blessing to proceed?"*

Wait for a response, similar to the last exercise (Connecting to Gaia). Does the Spirit of Place take a form in your Witch Eye? Check in with all of your clair-senses. Do they feel inviting and welcoming or do they feel hostile and unwelcoming? Sometimes the Spirit of Place will deny your request at that time without coming across as hostile. Respect whatever you receive. If you get the thumbs up from the Spirit of Place to proceed, you can engage in a psychic conversation with it, such as asking the Spirit of Place questions about it and its history.

Exercise 70

Scrying with Nature

A classic technique among many witches and Pagans is to scry with nature, and it's one of the easiest techniques out there. Scrying is the act of gaining clairvoyant information through meditative observation of an object, but in this technique, scrying is performed with nature as a whole. Usually, this technique is performed while casually strolling through nature or while sitting in a specific spot in nature. Before you begin you will want to have a single question in mind—it's okay if that question is simply "What do I need to know right now?"

Ensure that you're in a relaxed and meditative state. You can either activate your psychic prompt or perform the full Tuning In exercise. You may also choose to perform the last two exercises if the place is new to you. Whether you are walking or sitting in one spot, take in your surroundings in a passive manner.

If Spirit were to be conveying an answer to your question through metaphoric imagery of nature, what is the message? What animals, insects, or plants do you see? What is their behavior? Do the bushes, tree canopies, or clouds bring forth images or faces? How would this relate to your question?

When you are home you may also want to look up what the spiritual significance is of any animal, insect, plant, or symbol that caught your attention for a deeper layer of understanding.

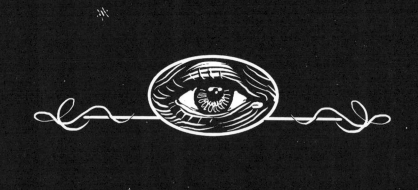

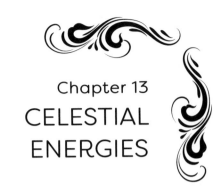

Chapter 13
CELESTIAL ENERGIES

Ancient occultists didn't just recognize the influence of Gaia. If Gaia was alive, surely the other planets were too, and therefore they too had some effect on us. Throughout human history, people have been tracking the stars and planets and recording their influence upon us. People recognized the archetypal energy that these stars and planets held and realized that their influence could be aligned with and harnessed in magickal endeavors. The ancients held seven planets to be of strong influences, which are the Sun, Moon, Venus, Mercury, Mars, Jupiter, and Saturn. You may notice that they viewed the sun and the moon as planets, which we don't today, and refer to them as luminaries. But the definition of a planet in ancient times was different.

The word "planet" comes from the Greek word *planētēs*, meaning "wanderer." A planet was defined as one of the principal seven objects that wandered in our sky. The Greeks named the planets because of their archetypal powers and named them after their gods. It's important not to get too hung up on or confused about the planets and their namesakes. In a lot of ways, the planets exert influences that are similar to these gods, but also differ in many ways. The celestial objects that are closer to us have a strong spiritual influence upon us, while those that are farther away have a decreasing influence upon us. While there have been more planets that have been discovered since the original Greek planets, the seven wanderers are the most powerful to work with in terms of magick and will be what we focus on.

These planetary influences are known as astral influences, the name itself referring to the celestial planetary realms. Another way to think about the planets and their influence and how they affect us, is to think of the solar system as a macrocosmic being, which each celestial object being a part of the whole.

Each planet has a glyph which is composed using combinations of the three main visual elements of the cross, the circle, and the crescent. The circle represents the spirit and is related to the Higher Self, the cross represents matter and is connected to the Middle Self, and the crescent represents the soul which is linked to the Lower Self.[40]

Planetary Correspondences and the Doctrine of Signatures

After the four elements, you will find that books on witchcraft will use the planetary powers as the next primary form of correspondences. You'll see lists of many plants or crystals correspond to different planetary energies. This system of correspondences came from the Doctrine of Signatures. The Doctrine of Signatures examines the shape, color, appearance, and the number of leaves and petals on a plant to determine what it does for the body or how it interacts with its environment. A clear common example is lungwort, which medicinally helps alleviate breathing problems and has leaves shaped like lungs.

The concept of correspondences is based on the Hermetic axiom of "As above, so below. As within, so without." In the first century Common Era, Dioscorides wrote *De Materia Medica* using this concept and applying it to plants. About one hundred years later the works of Galen embraced the notions presented in *De Materia Medica*, and Galen's work has been one of the main historical influences on modern medicine and health.

In the 1400s, Paracelsus expanded and enhanced the idea of correspondences when he and other alchemists and occultists saw that a plant's properties based on the Doctrine of Signatures were ruled by specific planetary powers. Therefore, the nature imbued in the spirit of the plant was thought to have the signature or correspondence with that planetary power and could assist in magickal endeavors surrounding things that needed that planetary power as they were already plugged into it.

---

40. Ivo Dominguez Jr., *Practical Astrology for Witches and Pagans: Using the Planets and the Stars for Effective Spellwork, Rituals, and Magickal Work* (San Francisco, CA: Weiser, 2016), 27–28.

Laurie Cabot explains this beautifully, stating that "Nature is particularly good at holding a pure light, a pure vibration. Humans are easily influenced by all of the planets and stars, and likewise everything else is too, but herbs, woods, stones, metals and animals have a very pure consciousness, a very pure aura, and are able to anchor specific vibrations from one or two different planets. We say that a magickal ingredient is 'ruled' by a particular planet or sign."[41]

As for the gender aspects used in older correspondence lists and charts, these ideas aren't related to our modern understanding of gender, and grew out of favor for other traditional terms such as "hot" and "cold" which better portrayed what the terms were trying to convey without the older sexist connotations. For example, stimulating, aggressive, electric, or positive is considered "hot" (formerly masculine). If a plant or herb is relaxing, passive, magnetic, or negative it is considered "cold" (formerly feminine). Such things are used to determine the "gender" of a plant's association. We even see this switch in the time of Cunningham; in one herbal book he uses gender and then in the next one he uses "hot" and "cold" and discusses why he's avoiding the gender terms from then on.

Correspondences are also based on how plants interact with the body or their environment. For example, wormwood is useful for dispelling parasites in the body, so it's also good at dispelling lesser beings outside of the body and the aura; all of this is a very Mars archetypal energy. Mugwort medicinally is calming and promotes sleep, which in turn are effects which encourage the pineal gland to produce melatonin, and in turn promotes more psychic ability; all of this is a very Moon archetypal energy. By using the Doctrine of Signatures, we can come to understand what the central archetypal planetary power of a plant or crystal is based on how it looks, which gives us insights into what it does medicinally. These medicinal properties suggest what they do magickally and spiritually.[42]

The main thing to take away from this is that everything upon our planet corresponds to a planetary energy, just as plants do, and that there's reasoning

41. Laurie Cabot with Penny Cabot and Christopher Penczak, *Laurie Cabot's Book of Spells & Enchantments* (Salem, NH: Copper Cauldron, 2014), 39–40.

42. Christopher Penczak, *The Plant Spirit Familiar: Green Totems, Teachers & Healers On the Path of the Witch* (Salem, NH: Copper Cauldron, 2011), 71–73.

behind these correspondences. By learning what that planetary power is, you can attune to that planetary power through psychic means and further activate its magickal properties and powers to work with it on a deeper level. I'll show you how in the next two exercises in this chapter.

The Sun

The Sun is the power of the spirit and symbolic of the Higher Self represented within our solar system. Its power is linked to the sense of identity and the self. It governs well-being in every area of self, including health, wealth, happiness, and prosperity. The glyph for the Sun is a circle of spirit with a dot in the middle. Ivo Dominguez refers to this as being symbolic of the relationship between the microcosm and the macrocosm and of spirit making itself manifest.[43]

 The glyph of the Sun can also be seen as a symbolic representation of the Sun itself. The Sun is also a star, and as such is the most divine planetary object in our solar system, being a direct manifestation of the Star Goddess. The Sun governs Sunday.

Tap in to Solar energy for magickal endeavors related to: advancement, ambition, confidence, creativity, dominance, egotism, expression, fame, fatherhood, friendship, greed, growth, happiness, healing, health, illumination, individuality, joy, leadership, life, manifestation, masculinity, motivation, personality, personal power, power, pride, prosperity, renown, self-esteem, sense of self, strength, success, vitality, wealth

Day of the Week: Sunday

The Moon

The Moon is the power of the soul and symbolic of the Lower Self represented within our solar system. Its power is linked to the realm of the hidden such as psychic ability, magickal prowess, emotions, instinct, glamoury, and

43. Ivo Dominguez Jr., *Practical Astrology for Witches and Pagans: Using the Planets and the Stars for Effective Spellwork, Rituals, and Magickal Work* (San Francisco, CA: Weiser, 2016), 28.

illusion. The Moon is one of the celestial bodies that is most intricately connected to witchcraft, aside from the earth itself. Witches work with different phases of the moon to assist in different magickal endeavors. The waxing moon phase is used for manifestation magick and the waning moon is used for banishment magick.

The glyph for the Moon is a crescent moon, being composed of a crescent. Shocking, huh? The Moon's energy can manifest and banish energies within ourselves and situations in our lives, through its waxing and waning.

Tap into Lunar energy for magickal endeavors related to: astral work, birth, compassion, divination, dreams, emotions, empathy, femininity, glamour, gratitude, family, home, illusions, imagination, increasing and decreasing, intuition, magickal prowess, motherhood, patience, psychic ability, shape-shifting, spirituality, subtlety, transformation

Day of the Week: Monday

Mercury

Mercury's power is linked to the realm of thought, speed, movement, communication, processing, business, and trade. The English words *mercenary* and *merchant* are derived from the Latin *Merx*, which is the same root as the Latin word for Mercury, *Mercurius*. The word *mercurial* is anything that relates to the planet Mercury, but also relates to the idea of swiftly changing one's stance, perspectives, or mind.

The glyph for the Mercury is the crescent of soul crowning the circle of spirit above the cross of matter. The glyph can also be seen as a symbolic representation of the Roman god Mercury's caduceus staff.

Tap into Mercurial energy for magickal endeavors related to: business, communication, deception, flexibility, healing, insight, intellect, knowledge, logic, magick, memory, mental processes, music, perception, poetry, protection, processing, science, speaking, studying, technology, theft, thinking, trade, travel, trickery, writing

Day of the Week: Wednesday

Venus

Venus is the power of beauty, receptivity, attraction, and fertility. While Venus tends to be associated with love and beauty, it also is linked to the realm of fertility and nature and also has a darker side, just as nature and beauty do. Many words are derived from Venus, such as *venefica*, which means "poisoning" and links to the idea of poisoning through plants and herbs, and the same goes for venom, which is related to venefica. "Venereal" pertains to the concept of love and pleasure, such as venereal diseases, which are sexually transmitted diseases. When we adore, worship, and love someone, we venerate them. There's also the link between wines and vines and Venus, deriving from a Proto-Indo-European root word *wen*, tying together the ideas of pleasure, intoxication, and the earth.

 The glyph for Venus is the circle of spirit above the cross of matter. The glyph can also be seen as either the hand mirror of Venus or a flower.

Tap into Venusian energy for magickal endeavors related to: agreements, attraction, affection, art, beauty, cooperation, culture, emotions, fertility, friendliness, friendship, grace, glamour, inspiration, jealousy, love, luring, luxury, passion, peace, pleasure, relationships, romance, self-confidence, sensuality, sex, sexuality, sociability, valuables

Day of the Week: Friday

Mars

Mars is the power of force, raw energy, physical strength, stamina, battles, confrontations, military, fighting, self-defense, and sexual potency. Mars energy can be beneficial when you need assistance in breaking things down or breaking through them. The word "martial" pertains to anything related to planet Mars but also is used to describe things pertaining to the military, such as martial law, or the martial arts.

 The glyph for Mars is the circle of spirit with an arrow of directed force, the only glyph to break the formulaic rules. The glyph for Mars can also be seen as a shield and a spear.

Tap into Martial energy for magickal endeavors related to: aggression, anger, battles, boundaries, conflicts, confrontations, courage, defense, disputes, energy, lust, motivation, passion, physical strength, protection, raw energy, releasing bondage, sex drive, sexual potency, stamina, strength, vengeance, vigor, vitality, war

Day of the Week: Tuesday

Jupiter

Jupiter is the power of higher truth and justice, leadership, wisdom, religion, faith, and expansion. The word *Jupiterian* pertains to anything related to ambition, leadership, and religion. Jupiter is also related to the idea of divine blessings, and as such, words like *jovial* (Jove being a variant of Jupiter's name) refers to the idea of having a good nature and being amused or pleased. When we're in alignment with our Higher Self, we are expansive, and areas of our lives begin filling with the blessings of wisdom, justice, and prosperity.

 The glyph for Jupiter is the crescent of the soul and the cross of matter. It can also be seen as the throne of Jupiter.

Tap into Jupiterian energy for magickal endeavors related to: abundance, ascendancy, authority, devotion, enthusiasm, ethics, expansion, fortune, growth, higher purpose, higher consciousness, honor, humor, justice, law, legal system, life path, luck, optimism, philosophy, morality, politics, prosperity, religion, responsibility, rules, rulership, spirituality, true will, truth, wealth, wisdom

Day of the Week: Thursday

Saturn

Saturn is the power of rules, restriction, contraction, shielding, protection, boundaries, evolution, endings, and karmic lessons. The word *Saturnine* relates to anything dark and gloomy. While Jupiter expands areas of life, Saturn restricts them. While Jupiter grows, Saturn harvests. While Mars is more aggressive in its energy, Saturn is more defensive.

 The glyph for Saturn is the cross of matter with the crescent of the soul. The glyph for Saturn can also be seen as the upside-down scythe of Saturn, indicating the scythe being used.

Tap into Saturnine energy for magickal endeavors related to: aging, agriculture, austerity, bindings, boundaries, death, destruction, duty, equilibrium, fear, formation, history, initiation, intimidation, karma, life cycle, life lessons, limitation, patience, perseverance, practicality, protection, prudence, responsibility, restriction, sacrifice, self-discipline, shadow work, teaching, time, wisdom

Day of the Week: Saturday

Exercise 71

Attuning to the Planetary Energies

Begin by tuning in and performing a soul alignment. Take a deep breath and state:

> *"I intend to vibrate in resonance with the power*
> *of [planet], so that I may know you."*

In the air before you, draw the glyph of that planet in blue Witch Fire and draw a clockwise circle around it. Feel the energy of that element emanating from your planetary portal. Feel the energy of the planetary power surround you. Perform the Lunar Breathing exercise, except focus only on the planet you are calling in replacement of the Moon in that exercise— unless of course, you're calling the Moon.

Take in the planetary energy, and let it charge and fill you. Visualize the glyph appearing on your chest and your body glowing with this energy, filling your body and aura with its energy. What does it feel like? What does it look like? What does it smell like? What does it sound like? What does it taste like? Perform this for each planet, starting with the Sun, and going through the Moon, Mercury, Venus, Mars, Jupiter, and Saturn, until you've become acquainted with them all.

Exercise 72

Conjuring Planetary Energy for Charging and Sending

Begin by tuning in. Activate your palm energy centers. Decide which planet you want to conjure. Draw the planetary glyph with the fingers of your projective hand on the palm of your receptive hand and draw a clockwise circle around it. Begin focusing on what the specific planetary energy feels like, based on your experiences from the previous exercise. Hold your hands apart. Visualize the glyph appearing on your chest and your body glowing with this energy, filling your body and aura with its power and then visualize them streaming out into each hand, creating an orb of energy formed purely of that element.

You can use this energy to charge objects with a specific planet. For example, if I wanted to charge a crystal with the planetary power of Mercury, I would take the Mercury planetary energy in my hands and place it around the crystal, visualizing all of that elemental energy filling and activating the crystal. You can also send this orb of energy to another person over distance. Solely focus on the energy orb inside of your hands, think of the recipient, and take a deep breath. Exhale forcefully, visualizing that you are blowing the sphere of elemental energy to its destination.

Chapter 14
MULTIDIMENSIONAL MANIFESTATION

A n aura is a field of energy that surrounds all objects, people, and entities. The more complex the being, the more complex the aura will be. For that reason, inanimate objects tend to have very basic auras. Rocks will have less complicated auras than plants. Plants will have less complex auras than animals. Animals tend to have less intricate auras than human beings. The aura appears as a field of colored light that conveys psychic information to us. Auras can tell us about the emotional state, moods, thoughts, health, and spirituality of a person.

The word *aura* comes from the Latin word *aura*, which means "a breeze." In Greco-Roman mythology, four gods personified the four cardinal winds. These gods were called the Anemoi. The Anemoi had daughters who were the nymphs of the breezes. These nymphs were called the Aurae. There was also the principal goddess of breezes who was named Aura. Aura and the Aurae were depicted in classical art as having a *velifactio*, which was a piece of fabric that would billow in the breeze behind them. This velifacatio would frame around them in an egg-shaped layer, which is reminiscent of how the aura looks to the eye.

The velifacatio represented celestial energy, or what we might call astral energy in modern times, as the word *astral* is derived from the Latin word *astrum*, which means connected to the stars. Later, the velifacatio would be depicted in art behind royalty and people of a certain quality of worldly power. This is similar to how halos are used in art to illustrate a holy person, which is also a reference to the aura of a person. I'm sure you've heard the expression that someone has an "air about them." This expression points to the idea of an aura that a person has.

The word aura is very similar to the word *aurora*. Aurora was the goddess of the dawn, and her name means "morning light" or "dawn." Aurora and Aura were conflated by Roman writers such as Ovid in "The Metamorphosis." I think this gives another layer of meaning to why we use the word aura for the energy field. So not only is it a non-physical "air" about a person that appears in layers, but it's also colored light just as the dawn sky is filled with various colored lights all blending into one another, just as the aura around a person appears.

The Cauldrons and the Auric Field

The three spiritual cauldrons are our inner portals of our auric field. Just as the image of a classical witch's cauldron is filled with a liquid which in turn steams and boils out, so too are our cauldrons continually taking in energy from different realms of reality and, when filtered through ourselves, are expressed as an auric field around us. The function is similar to breathing. We're always taking in information from our multidimensional energetic environment and filtering it through our inner cauldrons and releasing it as auric fields around us. Each cauldron processes two different dimensional bands of our reality. The Cauldron of Warming as a focal point of our Lower Self processes etheric and astral energies. The Cauldron of Movement as a focal point of our Middle Self processes mental and emotional energies. The Cauldron of Wisdom as a focal point of our Higher Self processes psychic and divine energies.

These auric fields act as our other bodies in our multidimensional reality. While our focus is predominantly on our physical bodies, we have six other bodies also existing within their own dimensional band of reality. Think of the dimensional bands of reality as channels of energy all existing within the same space. Just like radio waves, they're seemingly invisible and unperceivable, but if you use a radio and tune in to the right station by homing in to that radio frequency band, a specific radio station emerges. By working with our spiritual cauldrons, we can learn to tune in to these dimensional bands to differing degrees.

Therefore, the physical body is our body within the physical plane. Our etheric body is our body in the etheric frequency band. Our astral body is our body in the astral frequency band. Our emotional body is the body within the emotional frequency band. Our mental body is the body within the mental frequency band. Our psychic body is our body in the psychic frequency band, and our divine body is our body within the divine frequency band. These are all existing simultaneously, and our physical body is the nexus binding and holding these bodies together as a mortal coil.

These frequency bands are housed in a broader grouping that we experience as the three worlds in the World Tree. The Lower World of the roots of the World Tree houses the etheric and astral. The Middle World of the trunk of the World Tree houses the mental and emotional. The Upper World of the branches of the World Tree houses the spiritual and divine.

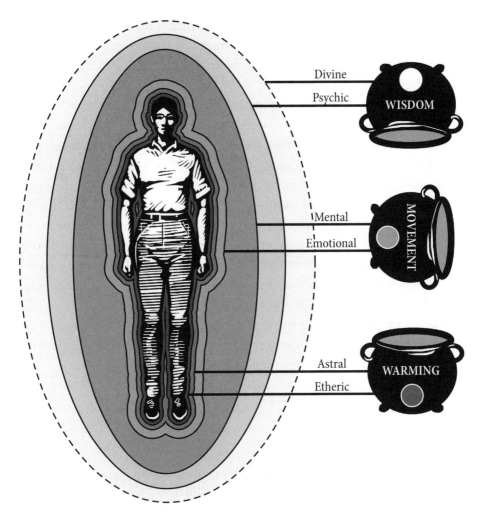

Figure 18: The Aura in Relation to the Three Cauldrons

Reality Maps

If you've read other metaphysical books, there's a strong chance that you've seen the aura and reality explained or depicted a bit differently. That's because when it comes to the realm of the spiritual, nothing is concrete, and therefore it's not a precise science. However, we can chart these into models that help us navigate in these realms by having a basic understanding of what is out there. Christopher Penczak refers to these as "reality maps" in the Temple of High Witchcraft,[44] and it's important to understand that reality maps are models created to serve a specific purpose. When we get too hung up on one particular model of ourselves or reality itself, we stunt our growth, what's accessible to us, and our possibilities. Likewise, I've discussed what beings you're most likely to encounter in these planes of reality; does that mean that this is where they concretely exist? Absolutely not. What it means is that this is where you're most likely going to be able to come into a sympathetic channel of resonance and be able to experience them.

So why are the auric fields depicted the way that they are if they're coexisting within the same space? Why is this division of the auric fields represented in the layer arrangement that they are? The first answer is that everyone's psychic perception is different. Think of each psychic as having a different level of zoomed focus. When a psychic looks at the aura they may see the layers rearranged in different ways and they may also perceive subtler distinctions or more generalized auric bodies. The second reason is that this particular reality map helps us understand which energies are tied to which parts of the World Tree along with our Three Soul and Three Cauldron Model. The most important reason, however, is that this order of auric layers and levels of reality helps us understand the mechanics of magick. It clearly charts out the steps we take in casting magick, how it goes from our physical reality to the divine, what steps we take to receive the manifestation, and how that magick is returned as results from the divine to our physical reality.

---

44. Christopher Penczak, *The Temple of High Witchcraft: Ceremonies, Spheres and the Witches' Qabalah* (Woodbury, MN: Llewellyn Publications, 2014), 69–75.

Multidimensional Magick

To perform successful magick, we start with the physical. We may gather physical ingredients such as candles, herbs, poppets, crystals, etc. We may even hold our physical prompt gesture of crossing our fingers. This begins the energy work. We then create an energetic container for it in the etheric by creating space for the magick. This is expressed as clearing the mind and getting into an altered state, setting aside a time to perform the magick, and casting a circle or creating sacred space. By doing this, we are setting the stage for creation. Next, we push that container of magick along with what's in it, which is often referred to as a thoughtform, into the astral by filling it with our willpower and willing our intentions to manifest.

We then push this thoughtform into the emotional by conjuring up and aligning with the emotional energy we wish to manifest and directing that into the spell. Rootworkers and conjurers are known for playing classical blues and jazz music, which evokes the emotional power of the working that they're doing, in the background while performing their magick. If you're creating magick to manifest love, you evoke those inner feelings of love and bliss to be attached to your thought form. We then move the thoughtform into the mental by expressing our desire clearly. This is done through mentally or verbally affirming what you desire, writing out a petition, speaking the words of a spell, chanting, or singing.

In the next stage of our magick, we push the thoughtform into the psychic by clearly envisioning the outcome we desire and visualizing how that desire may be manifested. The last step in our formula for casting a spell, we send it out into the Divine by petitioning deity to intervene on our behalf. This can be expressed as witches raising the cone of power and sending the thoughtform out into the cosmos to be done. We surrender the thoughtform to the highest levels of reality and release our attachment to it.

Once this is done and the actual magickal casting is finished, it then returns to us like a boomerang. It is returned to us by ensuring all of our energy is in alignment with what we are seeking to obtain. When every part of ourselves is in alignment with our magick, we become our magick and it is almost impossible for that magick to not become a reality. We honor the Divine and align with our Higher Will and we act in service to others, which initiates the manifestation back into our lives. From the Divine, it enters into the psychic as we envision that the spell has already manifested and happened, and refusing to envision any outcome that contradicts our desire.

From the psychic, it enters the mental by knowing that it is already being fulfilled and not allowing our thoughts that contradict our desire to override our manifestation. It then enters the emotional by feeling that it is happening and ensuring that we are emotionally optimistic about its manifestation. It's then brought down into the astral by remaining utterly steadfast in our willpower and refusing anything less than results. It then begins anchoring into the etheric when we create space within our lives for it to manifest.

It then becomes a physical reality when we take the initiative of action, which is an essential but often overlooked element in spellcasting. Physical activity is like creating an outlet for all of this energy to flow through into the physical plane. For example, you are not going to manifest the perfect relationship for you if you are not actively putting yourself into social situations where you can meet someone. If you've performed all of these steps but sit on your laurels, there's a strong chance that nothing is going to change nor is your soulmate going to burst through the walls of your living room only to find you on your couch.

The Etheric

The very first layer of the aura is called the etheric body. The etheric body is the most accessible layer of the aura to see and what people usually see when they begin to see auras. It appears as an outline around a person, ranging from a few centimeters to a few inches in width. At first, it will usually look either like a transparent substance like heat rising off of hot pavement, or as a white or greyish haze around a person. With time and development, the psychic witch will begin to perceive the etheric body in full color.

The word "ether" comes from the Latin phrase *aethēr*, which translates as "the upper pure, bright air" with etymological roots in the Greek words *aíthō* meaning "I burn, shine" and *aithēr* meaning "upper air." Aether, in Greek mythology, was a primordial deity who embodied the substance that filled the upper regions of the abodes of the gods which they breathed the same way humans depend upon and breathe air. This gives us a clue of the nature of this field, as metaphysical energy. Plato wrote that "there is the most translucent kind which is called by the name of aether" in his work *Timaeus*.

However, the most significant insight into the nature of this field is gained by understanding its name comes from ancient Greek alchemical sciences. Aether was the name given to the fifth elemental force that makes up reality, also known as the quintessence in Latin, and more commonly today in English as Spirit. Spirit is the divine elemental force which permeates and composes each of the four elements. It is for these reasons that I believe this field is called the etheric field. Everything that exists in physical reality has an etheric form. That's because it is the energetic matrix upon which physical reality takes shapes. The etheric body penetrates every particle that creates matter and is the force that acts as a container to hold everything together into a grid-like contour.

The etheric realm is simultaneously the first step of manifesting from the physical and the last stage of manifestation before reaching the physical. A great way to think about it is as similar to traditional photography. When a photographer takes a picture, the image is captured and imprinted on the camera film as a negative. This process occurs from the film capturing light in its crystalline structure and recording it. This negative is similar to the etheric realm in the sense that from it the actual photograph is developed, but until it does, it is only a transparent blueprint of the image that resembles, but is not quite, the image before the image goes through the exposure process. Just like a roll of film that absorbs light to be recorded into an image, the etheric field also has a magnetic quality to it and in our metaphor it is the last place of attraction before we receive our desired results. Think of the process of sending and receiving a manifestation as taking a photo. In this metaphor think of the camera as having a roll of film inside. You point the camera in the direction of the object that you want to capture and click the shutter button. It then absorbs light into itself to record an image to be developed later.

The etheric body exists within the etheric realm, both of which act as the liminal bridge between the physical and the subtle spiritual energies, translating information back and forth. The etheric, however, is not solely dependent or interconnected with the material. In rare cases in which a spirit is taking on a full visible form before your eyes, it is manifesting an etheric body to interact with the physical realm more concretely and is the closest it can come to the physical without the shell of physical matter. Likewise, it's the energetic vehicle we can craft ourselves to hold all the other energetic ingredients out into the Universe when casting a spell.

For this reason, I like to think of the etheric as being linked to the idea of sacred space. When we cast a spell as witches, the first thing we do is create a sacred space to work within. An old metaphysical trick to receiving manifestation is clearing out physical space within your life for the manifestation to anchor into physical reality. If all physical objects have an etheric field, it would only make sense that by clearing excess physical clutter we are allowing a space for a new etheric manifestation to develop as there are fewer etheric fields in the way. For example, if you're trying to manifest a job, you will need to create the room in your schedule for it to be fulfilled. Or in my case, in the process of manifesting this book I have cleared space in my schedule in which I have the room to be able to create this book through typing it up.

The Astral

The second layer of the aura is called the astral body. The astral body still retains a rough shape of the physical body, being the next layer out of the etheric body, which holds the energetic matrix of form. The astral body is usually psychically seen as swirling colors, looking like nebulous clouds of light. However, being next to the emotional body, it also can change form and shape-shift and has the unique ability to create an astral double of itself, or portions of itself, and detach from the rest of the energetic bodies.

The astral body is also referred to as "the fetch." Sometimes the fetch can broadly refer to the Lower Self. Sometimes the term fetch can apply to an artificial servitor spirit that one has created to do their bidding, created out of their own energy field. Sometimes the fetch can refer to the vessel the Lower Self takes on when shape-shifting into an animal while traveling in other realms, particularly in ecstatic journeying and out-of-body experiences. The astral body can move through the inner and outer realms of our reality and is the bridge between the physical and spiritual realms without any concrete concept of time and space.

The astral body is connected deeply to emotional energy, being next to the emotional body; however, these are emotions that are not necessarily logical or thought-based, but more based on an unconscious fight-or-flight safety mechanism. Think of the feelings of a very young child or a small animal, and you'll be getting close to the idea. This is also the body itself that is related to desires, needs, wants, and drives. Therefore it is also associated with willpower. The astral body is the part of us that dreams, and the dreamscape and astral plane of reality are pretty hard to distinguish if there's any distinguishing of them at all. When we dream, we are enacting and interacting with our desires, needs, wants, drives, stresses, and fears. It is our willpower and our unconscious emotions that are setting the stage and propelling us through the dreamscape unless we become conscious, lucid dreamers within the dream. It is this part of the energy body that understands and experiences archetypes, memories, and dream symbols.

The astral body is malleable and often, without channeling direct willpower, is unstable. This is why in dreams it's usually hard to see one's own hands or feet or reflection for long periods of time, if they're perceived at all. When astral projecting outside of the body, a duplicate is created. Think of this duplicate as an astronaut's suit. During an out-of-body astral projection experience, the mental awareness will split into two portions, one being the astral body around a person and the other being the astral double. This lasts for a few moments until usually the mental awareness connects with the double as a primary focus.

A typical experience when one is about to astral project, but something messes up, is that the person's mental awareness in their astral body connected to their physical will wake up while the body is asleep and not link to this astral double. It's as if instead of choosing the double as the primary focus, it will decide to remain with the person. This phenomenon is called sleep paralysis since the physical body is completely paralyzed, as it is every time we sleep so that we don't physically enact our dreams.

A common report with sleep paralysis is that there is usually a dark shadowy figure in the room. Sometimes this is reported as a hag witch, a monster, an alien, or a demonic entity. My personal belief is that it isn't any of these things, but instead that this is the astral double we would typically enter to astral project. Because the astral body is connected to primal emotions, desires, and fears, it is unstable in its form. When one wakes up to find their body paralyzed and sees a shadowy figure in the room, it's only a normal reaction to become scared and panic. Since the astral body surrounding the physical body and the astral body's double are intricately linked—being the same energy body split into two—our astral double automatically takes on our fears and panic and takes on a hideous form.

If you ever find yourself in this situation of sleep paralysis, I have found that staying calm is the best thing you can do. The more you panic and resist, the more terrifying the experience will be. From this state you have two options: you can re-enter your dreams, or you can wake yourself up. If you want to re-enter your dreams, try to remain calm and close your eyes while focusing on the swirling patterns behind your eyelids; this will usually do the trick. If, however, you wish to wake up, the preferred method to wake up is to direct your willpower to your toes and try to use all of that willpower to wiggle them consciously, breaking the paralysis of sleep. A more natural method is to scrunch your face as if you've smelled something rotten. The key is to focus on one small part of your physical body and not the whole thing. Another method to wake up is to try to cough, which is an action that the mind allows the physical body to do while dreaming, which will then give you a moment to regain control of your body.

I believe that it is the astral body part of the soul that gets fragmented through traumas and left in different places within time and space. It is these astral fragments that are called back in a process referred to as "soul retrieval," in which a magickal practitioner is luring back aspects of ourselves to be reintegrated for wholeness. Keeping in mind that the astral body is a part of the Lower Self, think of it very much like a scared or wounded animal or a child that runs away to avoid more pain and abuse. These are parts of ourselves that are hiding out of fear due to a traumatic event. Just like a scared animal or child, the witch performing a soul retrieval must gain these fragmented aspects of the self's trust and prove that it's safe to return.

The astral realm is where we experience and process information in a broader, more unconscious manner, transcending conscious thought. This layer of reality is thought to be the layer of reality in which we experience astrological influences, which affect our moods and interactions without ever being consciously processed. It was believed that the astral realm was composed of different energies of planetary and zodiacal influences that enacted their will upon people, and that the astral was the space between the higher realm of the gods and humans. These stellar influences were called "the celestial spheres" by the ancient Platonists. This is why it is called "astral," which derives from the Latin *astrum*, meaning "star," as it is referring to the heavenly influence of astrology. As such, it is also where we experience other spaces of reality as a place to interact with.

When it comes to manifestation in spellwork, this layer of reality is connected to primal willpower. What I mean by that is that it is the layer where we hone what our specific desires are for the spellwork. These primal desires are classified as the planetary powers. For example, if you want to cast a love spell, you would connect with the energy of Venus, the planetary power that governs love. So mostly this stage is about picking which planetary energy your will is aligned with for the outcome of your goal and vibrating in harmony with that planetary energy. When it comes to receiving our manifestation, we maintain this primal willpower desire and keep vibrating in accord with that planetary energy. So with the etheric layer, we've created space and a container for the energy of the spellwork, and with the astral layer we give it a charge of our planetary will and begin to separate it from our energy fields so that it can go out into the Universe for manifestation.

The Emotional

The third layer of the aura is called the emotional body. The emotional body is where the energy bodies begin losing their shape, being further removed from the etheric body of form, but close enough to hold a bit of shape. It appears very much like the astral body, being swirls of cloud-like colors and light within the aura. The emotional body is the bridge between the mental body and the astral body. It is also the bridge between the Lower Self and the Middle Self. As such, the emotional body can relay the information regarding the subtle energies and influences that the astral body detects and express that as feelings of intuition via physical sensations and emotional sensations, which the mental body can then translate into understanding.

On the other hand, a lot of our emotions are affected by our thoughts and thinking. The emotional body processes this and translates it down to the astral body. The emotional body is constantly shifting as we go through various emotions throughout the day. Emotions that we continuously feel without shifting them to another state, such as depression, begin to imprint the astral body and become more deeply rooted. In the case of trauma, a mental experience processed through the emotional body is sent down to the astral body, which can fracture and splinter it.

The emotional body can be trained and worked with through the mind's mental body. We can learn to use our thoughts to condition our feelings, as in the case of affirmations. We can also create states of emotional pain and suffering through repeated negative thinking, fears of the future, and regrets of the past. Being a part of the Middle Self soul, the emotional body understands time and space and can experience and reflect those perceptions. Through cleansing our emotional bodies of the Middle Self regularly, we can wash our astral body of the Lower Self.

In the Faery/Feri Tradition of Witchcraft, practitioners perform a cleansing ritual called Kala, which originates from the spiritual tradition called Huna. During Kala, water is used (which has resonance with the astral body) as a reciprocal for emotional energy we want to cleanse. Feelings that are thought of as more negative in nature—such as anger, shame, regret, or grief—are transferred into the water and the divine is invoked to purify and transmute as healing. The witch then drinks the water as a remedy for the deeper wounds that the Lower Self of the astral body is holding on to, to help heal and loosen up the stagnant emotions affecting how we interact, feel, and think.

The emotional body is also where we connect with others through relationships and how we feel with others. This is the aspect of the Middle Self's spider embodiment that connects us through emotional threads called aka threads in Huna. These threads are connecting two or more people through the emotional body. It is also the energy body that contains energetic cords and hooks in more toxic relationships. This is the part of the self that emotional vampires will drain energy from, by creating a cord with the emotional body and mental body and manipulating the two to gain their sustenance. Sometimes emotional vampirism is unconscious, and in some rare cases, it's conscious.

When it comes to manifestation in spellwork, this layer of reality is connected to how we emotionally feel. Primarily, it's how we want our desired manifestation to feel on an emotional level when we receive it. In these terms, we divide the emotions into two primary aspects—positive and negative. While this may seem like oversimplifying the spectrum of emotions that can be felt, this is basically what this process of spellwork is focused on. For example, if we're casting a spell to find a new job, we will want to feel positive about the spell and not feel doubtful, sad, or worried.

So energetically we've created a container for the energy, we've aligned with our willpower by connecting to a planetary power and separated it from our energy field, and now we're telling the spell if we want the manifestation to enact that planetary power positively or negatively. Most often, unless you are working malefica or a binding spell, you will want to charge it to be positive to receive beneficial outcomes. When receiving the manifestation, we want to put ourselves in a state of emotion that we believe we will feel when it is happening. For example, if you're casting for a job, you will want to feel excited, happy, grateful, and relieved just as you imagine that you will when you've obtained it.

The Mental

The fourth layer of the aura is called the mental body. The mental body loses its form and appears as an egg shape around a person. It isn't perceived as moving colors, but rather as a faint light, usually with a light golden or yellow hue to it. Geometric shapes and forms are created within the light of the mental body as the mind thinks different thoughts. Through a prolonged manner of thinking, these geometric shapes and forms can crystallize within the mental body as "thoughtforms" within the auric field. As such, these thoughts can either help or hinder us.

It is through the mental body that we can express ourselves and our unique identities. It is the speaker and the listener. It is the part of ourselves that has beliefs, ideas, dreams for ourselves and the future, ethical stances, and affiliations with groups. The mental body is the part of ourselves that we most closely identify with and understand and is the most identified with the Middle Self soul. In fact, it is that voice right now inside of your head that is narrating this text that you're reading and creating images based upon that. It understands itself as individual from others and has a concept of self through the ego. It is the true bridge between the Upper and Lower Self. It can translate emotional impulses sent from the astral body as intuition, and it can translate divine pulses transmitted through the psychic to be understood by the conscious mind. It thoroughly understands the concept of time and space and can reminisce about the past, plan for the future, process information in language, and hold abstract thoughts and philosophies.

The mental body as spider connects different ideas and thoughts to gain a bigger picture. It also can home in on details. It also connects people together as distinct others, through words and thoughts, conveying not only information about physical reality to another person but also the emotional intelligence of the Lower Self as well as the abstract ideas and philosophies of the Higher Self. It is this part of our energy body that can manipulate and move things through the different parts of the World Tree and what binds the three souls of a person together. The mental body can program and heal our emotions and thereby manipulate the astral body and Lower Self. It can also mentally direct meditations, visions, and journeying work to harness the psychic and divine bodies.

The term Theosophists called the mental body was the causal body. Causal literally means to involve causation. Causation is the act or agency of producing an effect. It points to the idea that the mental body can express, indicate, and create cause and in turn return effect into one's life. The mental body is seen as the veil of illusion, which separates us from the auric bodies of the Higher Self that understand its interconnectedness and oneness with all things. It was also viewed as the seat of the soul, the place where our conscious focus predominantly sits and is connected to the physical-mental faculties and processes of the brain. It is for this reason that both the frontal lobe, which controls reasoning, self-control, and decision-making (which I would identify with the mental body) as well as the pineal gland within our brain (which I identify with the psychic body and which receives psychic and divine information) have both been referred to historically as the seat of the soul.

When it comes to manifestation in spellwork, this layer of reality is where we give instructions and specify with clarity what we want. It's how we tell the spell what we want it to do. So if we've created an energetic container for our energy, charged it with our planetary power desire, separated it from our own field, and given it a positive or negative charge, the mental level is where we program all of this raw energy to have instructions. We do this by explicitly specifying what we want to manifest through written and spoken words chosen carefully.

For example, if we're looking to manifest money into our lives, we don't just intend to "have money." Remember, the intention isn't everything, and this is where we turn intention into a direct command of willpower. If we cast a spell to receive money, we may find five dollars in the pocket of some old jeans. That may not be what you truly wanted or needed. It's through language and thought that we could clarify, "I desire to have enough money to pay my rent and bills and still have $1,200 left."

When receiving the manifestation, we keep ourselves in a state of knowing that the spell has worked and that our desire will manifest to fulfill our request. We keep our thinking positive and don't second-guess or doubt the working, but instead maintain a state of mind of faith and knowingness.

The Psychic

The fifth layer of the aura is called the psychic body. The psychic body is an egg shape around a person and is usually perceived as a deep indigo background, similar to the night sky. This field is best thought of like a mirror that reflects information from the divine body. These bits of information are seen psychically as streams of prismatic light flowing through this part of the aura against the night sky acting as a mirror of the will of the divine body. The concept of light being information is an almost universal concept throughout all time among mystics all over the world.

From the psychic body, the mental body can take those "downloads" received and is able to process them. Think of it as the divine body having information it wants to send the mental body. The psychic body is where that information is compressed like a .zip file as a package of information that is available to be downloaded by the mental body, which in turn decompresses the .zip to process all the individual files. But the psychic body doesn't just relay information in one direction. Through visualization, spellwork, and prayer it uploads information as well.

The psychic body's function and physical counterpart is the pineal gland. Remember earlier when discussing brainwave states I said that Laurie Cabot believes that psychic information is unseen light and that the pineal gland receives this information and interprets it? This is the light it is receiving, those light streams flowing from the divine body into the psychic body. The pineal gland receives the information, and the rest of the brain then processes it.

Once it's processed, the information moves into the mental body of perception and understanding.

The psychic body doesn't differentiate between self and other as the mental and emotional bodies do. It is the first part of ourselves that is connected to a sense of unification with the fabric of existence, being the first layer that composes the Higher Self soul. As such, it can receive information on potentially anything one could want. However, since it has less perception of boundaries as well as time and space, it doesn't always relay information in those concrete terms, leaving the rational mind having to piece together the information in a linear fashion to the best of its ability.

The word *psychic* comes from the Greek word *psukhikos* which means "relative to the soul, spirit, mind." This gives us a clue to the function of this energy body. It is where the spirit or Higher Self soul or divine body interacts with the mental body. The Theosophical name for this energy body is the Buddhic body. This gives us even more insight into the nature of this energy body. The word *Buddhic* is named after the Buddha and relates to the idea of higher states of wisdom, and universal love in a state of oneness and detachment from the ego of the mental body and Middle Self.

When it comes to manifestation in spellwork, this layer of reality is where we envision what we want with clarity in an altered state of consciousness. We see it in our Witch Eye and give an image of the spell's possible outcomes. So if we've created an energetic container for our energy, charged it with our planetary power desire and separated it from our own field, given it a positive or negative charge, and programmed it with instructions, this is where we visualize how that manifestation may look and raise our consciousness and vibration to upload it to the divine body.

The Divine

The sixth and final layer of the aura is called the divine body. The divine body is psychically perceived as pure light surrounding a person and emanating around their body. This light emits from the star of the Higher Self soul. In some traditions of Feri/Faery, the Higher Self is depicted as a dove descending and conjures up imagery of the Holy Spirit. If you look at depictions of the Holy Spirit dove descending upon a person or a place, you will see the light emanate from it and engulf a person. This is the perfect depiction of the divine body, the radiation from the Higher Self soul.

The divine body is also known as the Ketheric Template. The word "Ketheric" refers to *Kether*, a Qabbalistic term used by ceremonial magicians in their map of consciousness, divinity, and reality called the Tree of Life. Kether means "the crown" in Hebrew and refers to the highest manifestation of consciousness that humanity can intellectually understand. It is the pure brilliance of the Divine as well as our connection to divinity. The divine body holds the divine template of our True Will, whether we choose to fulfill it or not within our lifetime, as well as our agreements and soul contracts that we make prior to incarnation. The divine body contains the Divine Wisdom and has the template for our life's path. In many ways, it is our individual and personal god self that is guiding our path, never having been separated from Source itself.

The divine body is also known as the Atmic Body. Atmic relates to the Sanskrit word *Ātmán* which means "soul; self; essence; breath." This is a massive clue to the nature of this energy body and its function. The concept of Atman in the Bhagavad Gita is simultaneously one's innermost true soul essence, as well as an omnipresent force that is eternal and has never incarnated. This ties into the idea of the Bornless One in the occult tradition of Thelema. The Bornless One is the aspect of the Higher Self that hasn't incarnated nor has ever left Source. In our model, the dove/owl would be the Bornless One, and the rays emitted would be our divine body which is our connection to the Higher Self.

This concept can be summed up by Feri/Faery Witchcraft Tradition founder Victor Anderson who stated, "God is self, self is God, and God is a person like myself."[45] Likewise the prophet of Thelema, Aleister Crowley, wrote into his Gnostic Mass Ritual, "There is no part of me that is not of the gods!"[46] Or perhaps it's best summarized in *Rogue One: A Star Wars Story* where the blind Jedi monk Chirrut Îmwe chants the mantra "I am one with the force, and the force is with me." All these statements show the connection and oneness of the divinity of self and the god that transcends self.

45. T. Thorn Coyle, *Evolutionary Witchcraft* (New York, NY: Tarcher/Penguin, 2004), 43.
46. Lon Milo DuQuette, *The Magick of Aleister Crowley: A Handbook of the Rituals of Thelema* (York Beach, ME: Weiser Books, 2003), 241.

When it comes to manifestation in spellwork, this layer of reality is where we send it off into the Universe. So if we've created an energetic container for our energy, charged it with our desire, separated it from our own field, given it a positive or negative charge, programmed it with instructions, visualized the outcome, and raised our energy and vibration, it is in this phase that we now align our inner divinity with our higher divinity or the help of external gods (who are interconnected with ourselves through the Higher Self) and surrender our desire fully. If we think of traditional spellwork where one is directing and aiming the Cone of Power they've raised, which is the swirling reservoir of energy generated within a magickal working, this step in the manifestation process is releasing it to the Universe to be fulfilled. When receiving the manifestation, our chances are greater improved when we honor the divine within ourselves and the divine in all others and are in alignment with our True Will.

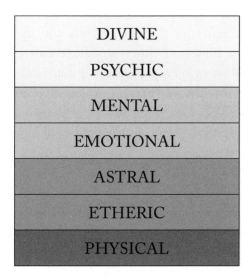

Figure 19: The Multidimensional Levels of Reality

Exercise 73

Multidimensional Mind Magick

Tune in and perform a soul alignment. Create an energy orb. Vibrate in harmony with the elemental energy that is appropriate for your spell's desire and fills your globe with that energy. Vibrate in harmony with the planetary energy that is appropriate for your spell's desire and fills your orb with that energy. Conjure the emotional energy that is appropriate for your spell's desire and fill your ball with that energy. Make a clear mental statement of the spell's purpose, visualizing the orb taking that as a command. Visualize what the spell will look like when it's manifested and direct that image into the orb by envisioning it having a short scene playing within it like a crystal ball in old movies. Focus on the energy orb inside of your hands and all that it's programmed with. Exhale forcefully, visualizing that you are blowing the spell sphere off into the Universe to manifest.

For example, if I'm casting a quick psychic spell to send healing to someone named Samantha who has the flu, I begin by tuning in and aligning my souls. I create an energy orb in my hands and focus on the elemental energy of Earth and allow it to fill my body for physical healing and infuse that energy into my orb. I then focus on the planetary power and glyph of the Sun, which rules health, and allow it to fill my body and infuse that energy and the image of the glyph into the orb. Next, I make a clear mental or verbal statement such as "It is my will that Samantha heals from the flu for the highest good of all." I see the words vibrate like a soundwave and enter the orb. After that, I visualize Samantha in perfect health and envision that image playing within the sphere. I take a moment to feel and visualize the energy strengthening in my hands, and I exhale forcefully blowing the spell off into the Universe knowing that it will manifest.

Exercise 74

Performing a Full Magickal Spell Ritual

This exercise can be physically performed or you can envision the whole thing within your Witch Eye. Either way the procedure is the same.

The formula for the spell is as follows:

1. Tune in.

2. Align your souls.

3. Perform an energy cleansing of the physical space.

4. Cast the circle.

5. Call the quarters.

6. Conjure the elemental energy you're using for the spell.

7. Conjure the planetary energy you're using for the spell.

8. Feel the emotion that you want the spell to have.

9. Make your statement of intent for the spell.

10. Perform the spell or working.[47]

11. Visualize what the results will look like.

12. Release the quarters.

13. Release the circle.

14. Close down.

Let me give you an example to help bring this home. Let's say I'm doing a spell to ensure that I have enough money to pay all of my bills. I begin as always by tuning in and aligning my souls. I make sure that the area I'm performing the magick in is physically clean and tidy before I perform an energy cleansing on the space. I cast the circle and call the quarters. I then focus on the element of Earth for abundance and fill myself with its energy and envision it filling the circle. I then call upon the planetary power of Jupiter for wealth, abundance, and expansion, and fill myself with its energy and envision it filling the circle. I conjure the emotions of how relieved and secure I will feel when the spell has manifested as if it has already manifested.

I make my statement of intent, saying "I desire to have enough money to pay my rent and bills and have $1,000 left over." I then proceed to perform the spellwork. When the spell is completed, I take a moment to visual-

---

47. See next chapter for examples of spells.

ize what it will look like by envisioning my bank account with that amount of money and writing checks for that amount for my rent and bills. I then release the quarters.

I tend to think of the magick circle like a giant cauldron of energy, a much larger version of the energy orb work where I'm infusing it with energetic ingredients and commands. My magick circle is now filled with all of the magick I've raised within, so it's time to release it out into the Universe. I release the circle, and as I do, I say:

"I cast this circle out into the Universe. As above, so below.
As within, so without. It is done. So mote it be!"

While saying this, I envision all of the magick rushing out into the Universe as a giant sphere. I then close down, putting extra emphasis on grounding myself.

Chapter 15
PSYCHIC SPELLS
AND MAGICK TRICKS

I t's my firm belief that magick can be utilized at almost any time if performed through one's psychic faculties and willpower, as long as one has a firm understanding of the elements necessary. We don't always have access to our altars, our tools, or our places of power. Sometimes we need magick in the moment. The following are some of the psychic spells and magick tricks that I perform fairly regularly to give you an idea of how everything in this book weaves together to create a foundation of enhancing your magick through your psychic ability and your psychic ability through your magick by uniting the two.

With all of these exercises we're going to assume that you have the other exercises down and that you understand what it means to tune in (which by now should be readily achieved by using your psychic prompt), how to connect and invoke each soul or perform a soul alignment, and how to attune to a planetary power. If the spell indicates that it's the Middle Self being tuned in to, you don't need to do anything special as it's considered our default setting. If for some reason you don't understand those preliminary steps, go back and read and review those steps thoroughly if you want the psychic spells to work effectively. Each spell will indicate which soul(s) you'll be invoking and connecting with and which planetary power to tune in to before you begin. I've also indicated which psychic abilities are being tapped in to and utilized in the spell itself.

Exercise 75

Absorbing and Imprinting Energy into an Object

Self Possession: Lower Self

Planetary Power: Venus ♀

Psychic Ability: Clairtangency

Do you ever wish you could "bottle up" a certain emotion or energy? A simple way to store energy is to awaken your hands and then hold an object in your projective hand that you want to use as the vessel for this energy, such as a crystal or charm, and using your receptive hand to conjure up the sensation that there's a whirlpool in your palm that's sucking in the energy or emotion that you want to contain. Draw that energy into your receptive hand and up your receptive arm and down your projective arm and imprinting upon the item in your projective hand. Feel the item receiving an aura about it of the energy that you're "bottling up." This is extremely helpful when you need a quick boost of energy such as love or self-esteem when you're feeling depressed.

Exercise 76

Boosting Offerings

Self Possession: Soul Alignment

Planetary Power: Jupiter ♃

Psychic Ability: Clairvoyance

This is a technique that I use to bolster offerings that I make to sweeten it further to their tastes and likings, whether that's offerings to spirits, ancestors, gods, or the land. Essentially what you want to do is envision that whatever you're offering has a smoke-like energy that is rising into the air, whether you're burning incense or offering another object like food or water. All you need to do to enhance the offering to be more pleasing is to envision items that the spirit enjoys as offerings or that are sacred to them rising up into the smoke. For example, let's say that I'm giving an offering to Hekate.

I place my hands above the offering and envision the energy rising up, carrying off things that are sacred to her. So in the case of this deity, I envision skeleton keys, saffron, garlic, and jugs of wine rising up in that smoke-like energy to her.

Exercise 77

❧

Clearing Out a Crowd

Self Possession: Middle Self

Planetary Power: Mars ♂

Psychic Ability: Clairvoyance

Do you ever want to clear out a space but don't want to be rude? Perhaps your guests are staying a bit longer than you want or there are unwelcome people in your environment? This one is my go-to secret trick. The beauty of this is that you never need to come off as rude or that you don't want the people around you, and no one will know what you're doing inside of your head.

I showed this to a coworker friend once to show them how effective it is. It was during October in Salem, and the witch shop that I was reading out of was beginning to close for the night at almost midnight, when suddenly about fifteen highly intoxicated people came into the store and began spreading out making fun of everything in the store with no intent of buying anything. I grabbed my coworker and went to the back of the store. I asked him if he'd seen Jim Henson's *Labyrinth* and if he remembered the scene in which Sarah and Hoggle are running down a tunnel trying to escape a horrifying drill that took up the whole space of the tunnel. He nodded and asked where I was going with this.

Being a bit of a show-off in the moment, I smiled and told him to watch. I attuned myself to Mars and proceeded to envision the drill coming from where we were in the back of the store all the way to the entrance of the store. As I did, wherever the drill was being envisioned the drunk visitors began walking away from it in one steady swoop until they were out the door.

If you're unfamiliar with *Labyrinth* (which is a shame), another good visualization would be from *Star Wars: A New Hope* where they're in the trash compactor and the walls are coming in at both sides to squash the characters. However, instead of visualizing the walls coming in at both ends of a room, just envision one coming from the back making the room smaller and smaller and pushing them out.

Exercise 78

❧

Communicating Clearly

Self Possession: Middle Self

Planetary Power: Mercury ☿

Psychic Ability: Clairgustance

Speaking clearly can sometimes be difficult, especially if we're sharing something deeply emotionally charged, we're speaking in front of crowds, we're interviewing for a job, or we're a bit shy. All you need to do after attuning to Mercury is begin to conjure up the taste of warm and soft honey in your mouth while you're speaking. You may even want to solidify this memory of the taste to conjure by tasting warmed up honey before you go out to speak.

Exercise 79

❧

Creative Thinking Cap

Self Possession: Soul Alignment

Planetary Power: Mercury ☿

Psychic Ability: Clairvoyance

This exercise is particularly handy when brainstorming for ideas and having epiphanies and revelations of a creative nature. After performing your soul alignment and attuning Mercury, sit down and close your eyes. Envision that you're wearing a hat. Some like to envision this as a steampunk hat with gears and such, while others opt for a more cyberpunk-looking hat that has more of a sci-fi computer feel to it, and some just like to envision a simple top hat. Regardless of what you pick, ensure that the vision of it evokes a feeling of boosting your mental processes. Envision on the top of your hat a lit lightbulb that is attracting new ideas. Spend a bit of time in contemplative meditation with a focus on what you're brainstorming, knowing that new creative ideas are coming to you.

Exercise 80

Drawing Something to You

Self Possession: Lower Self

Planetary Power: Venus ♀

Psychic Ability: Clairvoyance

This exercise can help boost any sort of spells you've cast or manifestation work that you're performing while you're out and about, and is best performed at the beginning of your day, every day until you've achieved your manifestation. Envision a symbol to represent your goal. Let's say that you're trying to manifest a new house. Tune in to your Lower Self, attune to Venus, and envision that you have a silver harpoon gun. See the symbol off in the distance and shoot your harpoon gun at it, envisioning a silver cord between you and it and seeing it slowly being drawn toward you.

Exercise 81

Enticing Others

Self Possession: Lower Self

Planetary Power: Venus ♀

Psychic Ability: Clairaudience

This is perfect if you're out looking for a date or you just want people to feel comfortable around you in general. After tuning in to your Lower Self and attuning to Venus, just conjure up the sound of a cat purring extremely loudly. Hear that purring surrounding and engulfing your whole aura and feel that energy of relaxation and enjoyment associated with a cat's purr. You'll quickly find how much more people are drawn to you, whether it's romantically or not.

Exercise 82
Enhancing Candle Spells

Self Possession: Soul Alignment

Planetary Power: Venus ♀

Psychic Ability: Clairvoyance

Here's a simple way that I enhance any candles that I use in spellwork. All you need to do after aligning your souls and attuning to Venus is look at the candle you're working with and add a visualization to the candle itself. For example, if you're doing a love spell, envision beautiful roses popping out of the candle and blooming. If you're performing a healing, you might want to envision a healing aura and halo around it. If the spell you're casting is for money, envision golden coins popping out of it. The possibilities are endless, but this simple addition of clairvoyance to candle magick really strengthens the spell you're performing.

Exercise 83
Finding Lost Objects

Self Possession: Middle Self

Planetary Power: Venus ♀

Psychic Ability: Clairvoyance

This is one that I use often, as I'm always losing stuff. If you're going out of your mind trying to find something you've lost, just take a deep breath and relax. Attune to Venus and hold an image of the object in your Witch Eye. In your mind call out to it:

"[Name of lost item], for you I yearn. Without hesitation, now return."

Envision the item glowing, rising up, and floating toward you. You may want to also pay attention to the scenery of where the object is when it begins to glow and rise up in your Witch Eye. This can often be a clue of where the item is, if not the exact location. If you can't find the item within ten minutes of searching, just repeat the process until you find it. The key to this one is to ensure that you're relaxed and not stressing out over losing the item. Stress blocks psychic perception.

Exercise 84

Good Luck Blessing

Self Possession: Middle Self

Planetary Power: Jupiter ♃

Psychic Ability: Clairvoyance

Need an extra boost of luck? Try this out the next time you hit up the casinos or buy a scratcher ticket. There's arguably no symbol associated with good luck more than the four-leaf clover, which is said to draw good luck to its owner. Attune to Jupiter (who rules luck) and envision a magickal four-leaf clover with a rainbow aura. Envision the four-leaf clover swirling around you leaving a rainbow trail that's enhancing your aura with good luck. Mentally or verbally state:

"Up and down, around and over. Good luck comes to me like a four-leaf clover."

Exercise 85

Heightened Psychic Receptivity

Self Possession: Higher Self

Planetary Power: Moon ☽

Psychic Ability: Clairvoyance

This exercise is helpful if you want to go deeper with your psychic session with clearer results. This is particularly helpful if you're performing mediumship or any sort of channeling. Invoke your Higher Self and attune to the planetary energies of the Moon. Envision that your mind is a clear crystal lake, completely pristine and still. See the full Moon above your head in your Witch Eye and envision its light and reflection appearing upon the crystal lake of your mind, knowing that your psychic receptivity and clarity is being enhanced.

Exercise 86
∽
Invisibility Cloak

Self Possession: Lower Self

Planetary Power: Moon ☽

Psychic Ability: Clairvoyance

This won't literally make you disappear before someone's eyes, rather it will make you less noticeable. Think of it more as a camouflage and a deflector. This is great for when you're in crowds and don't want to be noticed. I originally learned something similar from a friend when we were visiting a graveyard at night close to a residential area and didn't want to draw attention to ourselves. All you need to do for this exercise after tuning in to the Moon and the Lower Self is envision that you're wearing a grey cloak composed of mist. Hold in your mind the grey cloak of mist that covers you from head to toe. Hold in your Witch Eye that the cloak is refracting all the light and color around it and blending in with your surroundings.

Exercise 87
∽
Lie Detector

Self Possession: Lower Self

Planetary Power: Jupiter ♃

Psychic Ability: Clairvoyance and Clairtangency

This one will take some experimenting with another person to fine-tune your detector, whether it's face-to-face or whether it's through online chatting or phone. What you're going to do is envision that the person has their fingers in a polygraph lie detector and set your intention to feel a bodily sensation whenever they lie. I usually feel a slight buzzing or tingling sensation when I do this, but you might experience something a bit different. You will have the person tell you ten things, half of which are false. Ensure that the answers aren't too obvious.

After each statement, predict whether it's true or false and have them tell you if it was a true or false statement before moving to the next statement. Regardless of what your prediction was, conjure up the programmed sensation of the buzzing or tingling of a lie in your body whenever they say it was a lie. This is how you will fine-tune your lie detector. Keep repeating this exercise and you'll begin to notice that you can detect when someone is lying to you whenever you hold your psychic prompt, connect with your Lower Self, and envision their fingers connected to the polygraph machine.

Exercise 88

Money Magnet Multiplier

Self Possession: Middle Self

Planetary Power: Jupiter ♃

Psychic Ability: Clairvoyance

For this exercise you will need a dollar bill (or something equivalent based on your country). On a Thursday during a waxing moon, tune in and attune to Jupiter. Hold the dollar bill in your hand and envision it becoming magnetic. Draw the glyph for Jupiter somewhere on the dollar. Hold the dollar bill in your hands and envision money in every form that you can imagine being drawn to it. See dollars of every denomination, coins, checks, gold, jewels, increasing large bank account numbers, or anything you can think of all rushing to the dollar. Now fold the dollar up and place it somewhere in your wallet or purse where you won't spend it, near but separated from your other money.

In your Witch Eye envision every dollar in your wallet being charged by this money magnet dollar. Know that every dollar that you spend will be returned to you increased. While I don't suggest spending all your money on something frivolous, make sure that you're spending some of your money on things that you enjoy and that bring you pleasure and not solely on bills, rent, or mortgage. If you feel like the magickal effects of the Money Magnet Multiplier are weakening, take the dollar out and perform the working again on another Thursday during the waxing moon and draw another Jupiter glyph on the dollar. It's important to keep the same dollar for this working, regardless of how many Jupiter glyphs are on it.

Exercise 89

Psychic Substitutions For Materia

Self Possession: Soul Alignment

Planetary Power: Sun

Psychic Ability: All

Sometimes we just don't have an ingredient that we need for a spell. Do not fret! You can always summon the spirit of the materia that you're missing. For this, you want to attune to the Sun regardless of what correspondence the item you're missing is. The more familiar you are with the item that you're missing, the better, and if the item is a plant, make sure you know its scientific name.

For example, let's say that I'm creating an herbal blend that calls for various ingredients but I'm missing spearmint, the scientific name of which is *Mentha spicata*. What I would do is tune in and perform a soul alignment and then tune in to the planetary energy of the Sun. I would then call out to the spirit of spearmint by stating:

> *"I call upon the power and spirit of spearmint. Mentha spicata, come and join my working and lend your power to this spell."*

While calling out to the spirit of spearmint, I would engage every psychic clair that I can. I would conjure up its taste, smell, appearance, and feeling between my fingers and envision myself dropping the ingredient into the formula. You can do this with almost any item whether it's a crystal, a resin, animal fur, or whatever is called for that you just don't have access to.

Exercise 90

Recharging Your Magickal and Psychic Batteries

Self Possession: Soul Alignment

Planetary Power: Moon ☽

Psychic Ability: Clairtangency

We all have times when we feel completely off and may feel completely disconnected from our abilities and feel like nothing is working for us. It's completely normal and nothing to stress out about. Here's my remedy. For this exercise you will need a body of water like the shore of a lake, ocean, or a shallow stream. Perform this during a warm night. You will also want to know under what moon phase you were born, which a professional astrologer can help you find out or you can find out by looking it up online and entering your birth info into different astrology sites.

Water is conductive and receptive to magickal and psychic energies and the Moon rules both. While standing in the shallow water during that moon phase, perform your soul alignment and attune to the planetary energy of the Moon. Envision the moon's light falling all around you and blessing you. Don't worry if you can't see the moon or if you were born during a dark moon. Just visualize the moon sending you its energy. See the energy as white with silver sparkles. Proclaim:

"I align with the Moon on this night, to recharge my magickal birthright.
I align with the Moon on this night, to recharge my Witch's Sight.
One and the same, me and the Moon. I am fully replenished by lunar boon."

Exercise 91

Removing a Curse on an Item

Self Possession: Soul Alignment

Planetary Power: Saturn ♄

Psychic Ability: Clairvoyance and Clairtangency

Removing a curse or really negative energy from an item is usually less difficult than it sounds unless the person who cursed the item was an extremely skilled witch. Simply perform a soul alignment and conjure your Witch Fire. Attune to Saturn and hold the item in your hand envisioning it being engulfed in your Witch Fire. Now in your Witch Eye turn the fire from its electric blue color to a vibrant violet. The violet Witch Fire will burn away all curses, impurities, and negative energy attached to the item. In your Witch Eye see the flame burning the curse around the item to ash. See the ash being burned to nothing. While performing this, keep repeating the chant:

"The curse is lifted, the energy has shifted."

If you feel that it's yourself or another that has the curse upon them, you can perform this on the self or another instead of an object.

Exercise 92

To Be Left Alone

Self Possession: Lower Self

Planetary Power: Saturn ♄

Psychic Ability: Clairaudience

Sometimes you just want to be left alone and come across as threatening. This is one that I teach people to use when going through dangerous or sketchy neighborhoods or when they're walking to their car alone late at night. In many ways this is the reverse version of Enticing Others. After tuning in to your Lower Self and attuning to Saturn, just conjure up the sound of the most vicious dog growling and barking extremely loudly. Hear that barking surrounding and engulfing your whole aura and really tune in to the sense that others shouldn't mess with you.

Exercise 93

Warding an Item

Self Possession: Middle Self

Planetary Power: Saturn ♄

Psychic Ability: Clairtangency and Clairvoyance

Don't want someone to touch a specific item of yours? Maybe it's your journal or Book of Shadows. Sometimes protecting an item isn't enough. Sometimes you want to make the item seem really unappealing to them if they touch it. For this one you want to combine it with the Psychic Password (exercise 47). The trick that I use to make things of mine that are important seem unappealing is to attune myself to Saturn and then hold the item and conjure the image of it growing thorns all around it, along with the feeling of being pricked by the thorns. Really conjure up the feeling of how bad it hurts to touch the item. Lock this feeling and imagery with your Psychic Password and use it to unlock the ward.

CONCLUSION

It is my sincere hope that this book has provided you with the knowledge and experience to tap in to your psychic ability and magickal power, and use both for your advantage. There's often debate about authenticity when it comes to witchcraft and psychic ability. Sometimes cynical witches will sneer at others for "role-playing" as witches or say that they're lost in their imaginations. Pay them no mind. This is why the first exercise of the book includes role-playing and places emphasis on immersing oneself in one's own imagination—to show how powerful imagination enlivened with willpower is.

The importance of imagination has been highlighted by witches, occultists, psychics, and mystics throughout all the ages. Yet in our modern era where the imagination is frowned upon, emphasis on engaging the imagination and experimenting in magick is being casually brushed aside in favor of secular atheism, and even in witchcraft, for dogmatic practices. The author and Magister of the *Cultus Sabbati* beautifully writes that, "The Inner Nature of Witch-Cult is such that it has long recognised Imagination as one of the greatest incarnative powers of Man. This faculty, especially in the past four centuries, has been suppressed, manacled, muted, and assaulted in the profane order; content to atrophy in the Station of the Ape, it is thus become, in our present era, a Forbidden Art."[48]

Magick is often defined as a science and an art. The science aspect reflects the magickal underpinnings and mechanics that create successful change.

---

48. Daniel Schulke, *Lux Haeresis: The Light Heretical* (Hercules, CA: Xoanan, 2011), 72.

The art aspect is the personal interpretation and application of that science. Witchcraft is never cookie-cutter. Like recipes from a book, the recipes are often tailored to individual tastes as long as the general formula and steps are understood. I encourage you to experiment with the material in this book and make it your own. Make it reflect your own beliefs and ideals. Alter them based on new experiences and experiments. Create new techniques based on the elements provided. Your imagination is the limit and what will keep witchcraft ever evolving as we proceed into the future. Your magick should be as uniquely personal as you are as a person.

I hope that you have gained a new lens through which to view and experience the world around you. There's no problem that you don't have the inner solutions or tools to solve. The power is within you and will only grow stronger the more you use it. By being aware of what is within you, you can begin to alter your life and your surroundings to be more in alignment with the masterpiece you are creating. Your life is your own magnum opus in the crafting. It will not be perfected overnight. We *practice* magick and *practice* witchcraft, because we are honing and perfecting it, like any talent. The only limitations you have are those that you allow to be placed upon you.

BIBILIOGRAPHY

Anonymous. *The Kybalion: Hermetic Philosophy by Three Initiates.* Chicago, IL: The Yogi Publication Society, 1912.

Belanger, Michelle. *The Psychic Energy Codex: A Manual for Developing Your Subtle Senses.* San Francisco, CA: Weiser, 2007.

Brennan, Barbara. *Light Emerging: The Journey of Personal Healing.* Broadway, NY: Bantam, 1993.

Bruce, Robert. *Astral Dynamics: A New Approach to Out-of-Body Experiences.* Charlottesville, VA: Hampton Roads Publishing, 1999.

Cabot, Laurie, with Penny Cabot and Christopher Penczak. *Laurie Cabot's Book of Shadows.* Salem, NH: Copper Cauldron, 2015.

———. *Laurie Cabot's Book of Spells & Enchantments.* Salem, NH: Copper Cauldron, 2014.

Cabot, Laurie, and Tom Cowan. *Power of the Witch: The Earth, the Moon, and the Magical Path to Enlightenment.* New York, NY: Delta, 1989.

Coyle, T. Thorn. *Evolutionary Witchcraft.* New York, NY: Tarcher/Penguin, 2004.

Crowley, Aleister. *The Book of the Law.* San Francisco, CA: Weiser, 1976.

———. *The Book of Thoth.* York Beach, ME: Weiser Books, 2004.

Dominguez, Ivo, Jr. *Practical Astrology for Witches and Pagans: Using the Planets and the Stars for Effective Spellwork, Rituals, and Magickal Work.* San Francisco, CA: Weiser. 2016.

———. *The Keys to Perception: A Practical Guide to Psychic Development.* Newburyport, MA: Weiser Books, 2017.

DuQuette, Lon Milo. *The Magick of Aleister Crowley: A Handbook of the Rituals of Thelema.* York Beach, ME: Weiser Books, 2003.

Faerywolf, Storm. *Betwixt and Between: Exploring the Faery Tradition of Witchcraft.* Woodbury, MN: Llewellyn Publications, 2017.

———. *Forbidden Mysteries of Faery Witchcraft.* Woodbury, MN: Llewellyn Publications, 2018.

Foxwood, Orion. *The Candle and the Crossroads: A Book of Appalachian Conjure and Southern Root-Work.* San Francisco, CA: Weiser Books, 2015.

———. *The Flame in the Cauldron: A Book of Old-Style Witchery.* San Francisco, CA: Weiser Books, 2015.

———. *Tree of Enchantment: Ancient Wisdom and Magic Practices of the Faery Tradition.* San Francisco, CA: Weiser Books, 2008.

Fries, Jan. *Visual Magick: A Manual of Freestyle Shamanism.* Oxford, UK: Mandrake, 1992.

Gardner, Gerald. *The Meaning of Witchcraft.* York Beach, ME: Weiser Books, 2004.

Gass, George H., and Harold M. Kaplan, eds. *Handbook of Endocrinology, Second Edition, Volume 1.* Boca Raton, NY: CRC Press, 1996.

Grimassi, Raven. *Communing with the Ancestors: Your Spirit Guides, Bloodline Allies, and the Cycle of Reincarnation.* Newburyport, MA: Weiser Books, 2016.

———. *Encyclopedia of Wicca & Witchcraft.* St. Paul, MN: Llewellyn Publications, 2003.

————. *Grimoire of the Thorn-Blooded Witch: Mastering the Five Arts of Old World Witchery.* San Francisco, CA: Weiser Books, 2014.

————. *Old World Witchcraft: Ancient Ways for Modern Days.* San Francisco, CA: Weiser, 2011

Hauck, Dennis William. *The Complete Idiot's Guide to Alchemy.* New York, NY: Alpha Books, 2008.

Hunter, Devin. *The Witch's Book of Mysteries.* Woodbury, MN: Llewellyn Publications, 2019.

————. *The Witch's Book of Power.* Woodbury, MN: Llewellyn Publications, 2016.

————. *The Witch's Book of Spirits.* Woodbury, MN: Llewellyn Publications, 2017.

Jung, Carl Gustav. *The Collected Works of C.G. Jung: Volume 9, Part II, AION: Researches into the Phenomenology of the Self.* Princeton, NJ: Princeton University Press, 1959.

————. *The Collected Works of C.G. Jung: Volume 13: Alchemical Studies.* Princeton, NJ: Princeton University Press, 1983.

Kaye Sawyer, Irma. *The Brightstar Empowerments: Compilation Edition.* Self-published, 2016.

Lévi, Éliphas. *Transcendental Magic.* York Beach, ME: Weiser Books, 2001.

Locklove, James. *Gaia, a New Look at Life on Earth.* Oxford, NY: Oxford University Press, 1995.

Miller, Jason. *The Elements of Spellcrafting: 21 Keys to Successful Sorcery.* Newburyport, MA: Weiser, 2017.

————. *Protection and Reversal Magick: A Witch's Defense Manual.* Franklin Lakes, NJ: New Page, 2006.

————. *The Sorcerer's Secrets: Strategies in Practical Magick.* Franklin Lakes, NJ: New Page, 2009.

Nema. *The Priesthood: Parameters and Responsibilities*. Cincinnati, OH: Back Moon Publishing, 2008.

Niedermeyer, Ernst, and Fernando Lopes Da Silva. *Electroencephalography: Basic Principles, Clinical Applications, and Related Fields, Fifth Edition*. Philadelphia, PA: Lippincott Williams & Wilkins, 1996.

Orapello, Christopher, and Tara Love Maguire. *Besom, Stang & Sword: A Guide to Traditional Witchcraft, the Six-Fold Path & the Hidden Landscape*. Newburyport, MA: Weiser Books, 2018.

Oschman, James L. *Energy Medicine: The Scientific Basis*. Dover, NH: Elsevier, 2016.

Pascal, Eugene. *Jung to Live By: A Guide to the Practical Application of Jungian Principles for Everyday Life*. New York, NY: Warner Books, 1992.

Penczak, Christopher. *The Inner Temple of Witchcraft: Magick, Meditation and Psychic Development*. Woodbury, MN: Llewellyn Publications, 2002

———. *Instant Magick: Ancient Wisdom, Modern Spellcraft*. Woodbury, MN: Llewellyn Publications, 2006.

———. *The Outer Temple of Witchcraft: Circles, Spells and Rituals*. Woodbury, MN: Llewellyn Publications, 2004.

———. *The Plant Spirit Familiar: Green Totems, Teachers & Healers On the Path of the Witch*. Salem, NH: Copper Cauldron, 2011.

———. *The Shamanic Temple of Witchcraft: Shadows, Spirits, and the Healing Journey*. Woodbury, MN: Llewellyn Publications, 2005.

———. *The Temple of High Witchcraft: Ceremonies, Spheres and The Witches' Qabalah*. Woodbury, MN: Llewellyn Publications, 2014.

———. *The Three Rays: Power, Love and Wisdom in the Garden of the Gods*. Salem, NH: Copper Cauldron Publishing, 2010.

Plato. *Phaedrus*. Edited by R. Hackforth. Cambridge: Cambridge University Press, 1972.

Rankine, David, and Sorita d'Este. *Practical Planetary Magick: Working the Magick of the Classical Planets in the Western Mystery Tradition.* London, UK: Avalonia, 2007.

RavenWolf, Silver. *MindLight: Secrets of Energy, Magick & Manifestation.* Woodbury, MN: Llewellyn Publications, 2006.

———. *The Witching Hour: Spells, Powders, Formulas, and Witchy Techniques that Work.* Woodbury, MN: Llewellyn Publications, 2017.

Regardie, Israel. *The Golden Dawn: A Complete Course in Practical Ceremonial Magic.* St. Paul, MN: Llewellyn, 2003.

Salisbury, David. *A Mystic Guide to Cleansing & Clearing.* Winchester, UK: Moon Books, 2016.

Schulke, Daniel. *Lux Haeresis: The Light Heretical.* Hercules, CA: Xoanan, 2011.

Starhawk. *The Spiral Dance: A Rebirth of the Ancient Religion of the Goddess: 20th Anniversary Edition.* New York, NY: HarperCollins, 1999.

Wachter, Aidan. *Six Ways: Approaches & Entries for Practical Magic.* Albuquerque, NM: Red Temple Press, 2018.

Zakroff, Laura Tempest. *Weave the Liminal: Living Modern Traditional Witchcraft.* Woodbury, MN: Llewellyn Publications, 2019.

INDEX

T

V

W

To Write to the Author

If you wish to contact the author or would like more information about this book, please write to the author in care of Llewellyn Worldwide Ltd. and we will forward your request. Both the author and publisher appreciate hearing from you and learning of your enjoyment of this book and how it has helped you. Llewellyn Worldwide Ltd. cannot guarantee that every letter written to the author can be answered, but all will be forwarded. Please write to:

Mat Auryn
℅ Llewellyn Worldwide
2143 Wooddale Drive
Woodbury, MN 55125-2989

Please enclose a self-addressed stamped envelope for reply,
or $1.00 to cover costs. If outside the U.S.A., enclose
an international postal reply coupon.

Many of Llewellyn's authors have websites with additional
information and resources. For more information,
please visit our website at http://www.llewellyn.com.